VILLAGE OF PAINTERS

VILLAGE OF
PAINTERS

Narrative Scrolls from West Bengal

FRANK J. KOROM

PHOTOGRAPHS BY PAUL J. SMUTKO

MUSEUM OF NEW MEXICO PRESS   SANTA FE

Project editor: Mary Wachs
Manuscript editor: Rosemary Carstens
Design and Production: Deborah Flynn Post
Map: Deborah Reade
Composition: Set in Adobe Caslon and Cochin
Manufactured in: China
10 9 8 7 6 5 4 3 2 1

Library of Congress Cataloging-in-Publication Data

Korom, Frank J.
Village of painters : narrative scrolls from West Bengal / by Frank J. Korom ;
photographs by Paul J. Smutko.
p. cm.
Issued in connection with an exhibition held Oct. 29, 2006-Apr. 29, 2007,
Museum of International Folk Art, Santa Fe, New Mexico.
Includes bibliographical references.
ISBN-13: 978-0-89013-489-4 (pbk., jacket : alk. paper)
1. Folk art—India—West Bengal—Exhibitions. 2. Narrative painting,
Indic—India—West Bengal—Exhibitions. 3. Scrolls, Indic—India—West
Bengal—Exhibitions. 4. Juang (Indic people)—India—West Bengal—Exhibitions.
5. Scrolls—New Mexico—Santa Fe—Exhibitions. 6. Museum of International Folk
Art (N.M.)—Exhibitions. I. Title.
NK1048.W4K67 2006
745.0954'14—dc22
2006009095

Museum of New Mexico Press
Post Office Box 2087 Santa Fe, New Mexico 87504
www.mnmpress.org

édes Anyámnak és Apámnak

CONTENTS

*Kulasan Chitrakar performing
a scroll about social awareness.*

ACKNOWLEDGMENTS

In 1982, while still a graduate student, I met my first scroll painter; I knew then that a project of this sort would be worthwhile. I am extremely grateful to Joyce Ice and the staff at the Museum of International Folk Art for seeing the value in drawing attention to the tradition of Bengali narrative scroll painting and enthusiastically supporting it. Paul Smutko, the collections manager at the museum, especially deserves a note of gratitude for taking time off from his busy schedule to spend a month in West Bengal with me to take the photographs included here. Laurel Seth and the board of the International Folk Art Foundation also deserve thanks for their interest and financial support. At the Museum of New Mexico Press, I would like to thank Mary Wachs for her editorial expertise and Deborah Flynn Post for producing this aesthetically handsome volume. Thanks also to Rosemary Carstens of Carstens Communications for carefully reading the text and making valuable comments on how to tighten and improve it. Her efforts have made it a better read. I also wish to thank Mary Lawler and John Vorhees for their hospitality during several stays in Santa Fe as the planning for the project was moving forward.

The fieldwork upon which this book and the accompanying exhibition are based started in the winter of 2001 and was supported by a seed grant from the American Academy of Religion. The International Folk Art Foundation funded two more trips in the winter of 2002 and the summer of 2003, during which a wonderful collection of scroll paintings was assembled. I was fortunate to receive a Fulbright Senior Research Fellowship to support a sabbatical in India during the 2004–2005 academic year, which enabled me a substantial period of unfettered time to complete the research and to begin thinking about how to present the fruits of my labor. In Kolkata [Calcutta], I thank Mandira Bhaduri for her hours of hard work transcribing the Bengali songs that I recorded and Madhumita Saha (now in Boston) for consulting on some of the song translations. I also wish to thank Aditi Sen, then manager of the Kolkata branch of the American Institute of Indian Studies, for facilitating my first stay in the "village of painters." Nandita Palchowdhury of the West Bengal Crafts Council deserves thanks as well for sharing her knowledge of the Patuas and Bengali folk art in general. Iti Sarkar repeatedly provided stimulating conversations and delicious food, while Abhijit Ghosh, in his untiring comradeship, kept my spirits up when I was down. In Naya, Basanta Ghorai and his family served as cheerful hosts during my numerous stays. Lastly, to the Patua community I say *koti, koti pranam*![1]

---

[1] To make the text more accessible to the general reader, I have not used diacritical marks for Bengali terms, and Bengali words appear in italics only upon first occurrence.

Scroll painter Shyamsunder Chitrakar.

THE PATUA'S CREED

To speak the truth is our vow.
Our work will be to establish the truth.
We shall follow the path trodden by great men and women.
We shall serve the poor and downtrodden.
That will be our religion.

We shall speak the truth and not uphold the wrong.
It will spread the fragrance, the fragrance of the rose.

We will behave like human beings, not hating one another.
We shall light the way of truth, the light of truth will spread.

We shall overcome all malice and greed, all anger and lust.
To speak the truth is our vow.

Our work will be to establish the truth.
We shall follow the path trodden by great men and women.
We shall persuade men and women to act in a humane way,
To give up what is false in word and deed.

As the sunlight that shines on the daytime,
May we all become the light of goodness to everyone.

We shall honor those who are poor and oppressed.
Never shall we be unmindful of their sorrow.

We shall shun violence, speaking ill of others,
And spreading rumors.
To speak the truth is our vow,
And to follow the path trodden by great men and women.

— Nanigopal Chitrakar, Naya village, Medinipur, West Bengal. The Patua's Creed
was written as a way to legitimize the social status of the West Bengali scroll painters.

ITINERANT SCROLL PAINTERS
OF WEST BENGAL

On a misty morning in December of 2001, I boarded the crowded Medinipur local train at Howrah Station in Kolkata well before the sun rose. Roughly three hours later, after making virtually every stop on the line, I arrived in Balichak, a bustling frontier market town that serves as the hub for travelers to the interior villages of western Medinipur District. I then boarded an overcrowded local bus to take me on the final thirteen-kilometer bumpy ride to reach Naya, my ultimate destination. Having never been to the village before, I had to rely on the conductor to tell me when we would arrive. Roughly forty-five minutes later he shouted for me to push my way from the back of the bus, where I was standing pressed against a stack of baskets containing live chickens, to alight. Squeezing my way through the human and nonhuman obstacles in my path, I finally managed to get out and collect my suitcase from the roof of the bus, where a number of people sat who had been unable to find space inside.

The main road in Balichak, a railhead and market town in West Bengal.

Naya's main road viewed from one of the two tea stalls in the village.

The local hat *(bazaar) where Naya residents must go to buy fresh produce on a daily basis.*

My first impression of Naya was of a sleepy, agricultural village. As the bus noisily departed, I found myself standing on a dusty, semipaved road lined with tea stalls and a variety of small shops selling cloth, medicine, everyday goods, sweets, some fruits and vegetables, cigarettes, betel nuts, and fish, as well as businesses providing basic services like bicycle, wristwatch, radio, and television repairs and haircuts. For anything more, residents of Naya traveled to a nearby bazaar three kilometers down the road, where they could also catch the latest Bollywood film at the local cinema hall.

Although I had a contact in the village, we had never met, only spoken by telephone. Foreigners generally do not venture into the hinterlands of West Bengal, so my presence naturally drew the attention of everyone sitting in the tea stalls. Before I could get my bearings, a stout young fellow with red betel-stained teeth and lips wearing a blue-checkered *lungi* (male sarong) quickly sidled up to me and said, "Yes, going where?" These, I would later learn, were three of the approximately twenty-five English words my soon-to-be friend could utter confidently. I replied in Bengali that I was looking for the house of Master *mashai* (schoolmaster), who was expecting me to arrive before lunch. We introduced ourselves, and I learned that this young man's name was Gurupada. He asked me where I was from, and when I replied "America," he exclaimed proudly, "*Accha* (Oh, really), I've been there myself." I then asked him where, and he told me it was named Philadelphia, which happens to be the city where I did my graduate studies years earlier. Intrigued that this man who spoke almost no English had traveled to the east coast of the United States, I asked him if he would like to join me for a glass of tea. We seated ourselves in one of the tea stalls as every ear in the vicinity tuned in to our blossoming conversation.

After some trivial *adda* (gossip) to pass the time until the tea arrived, Gurupada asked me to explain why on earth I was in Naya, of all places. I told him I was there to study with the Patuas, a caste of itinerant scroll painters unique to greater Bengal. "*Accha*," he said again. "I am a Patua." I now suddenly felt the world shrinking around me. What are the chances that someone living in Boston who studied in Philadelphia would accidentally run into a Patua in a rural Bengali village who had also been to Philadelphia? It was now becoming clearer to me

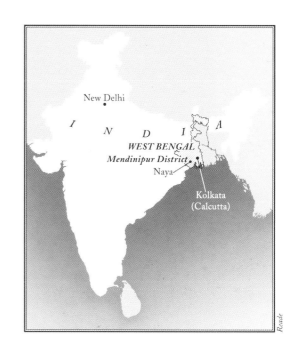

A spice and incense vendor in the local hat.

that it was his traditional occupation as a painter and singer that had motivated his American visit. I soon learned he had been invited by the North American Bengali Conference to be a part of the festivities surrounding an exhibition in King of Prussia on the outskirts of Philadelphia on Bengali art (Ghosh 2003, 845). I told him I met my first Patua in Philadelphia, when I volunteered to help out with the Festival of India tour that moved through the city in the fall of 1985. We both giggled at this strange concurrence of events, and found we even had some common acquaintances in India and the United States. Gurupada and I quickly

Gurupada Chitrakar enjoying a cigarette on a winter afternoon in 2004.

Three generations of the relatively affluent Ghorai family formally posing in their backyard.

became friends, realizing that our destinies were intertwined. I went on to explain that I wanted to learn everything I could about his caste's occupation, and he readily agreed to be my consultant.

After our tea, we walked down the road to the schoolmaster's house, where I was to stay for varying periods of time between 2001 and 2005. Basanta Ghorai's family belongs to the higher Mahishya caste that claims to be the original Bengali agriculturalists. As a result, he is more affluent than many in the village, lives in a double-story concrete, brick, and plaster house, and owns enough land to allow him to do some cash cropping to supplement his salary as a school administrator.

After eating the noonday meal, I took the customary rest but could not nap because a steady stream of Patuas came inquiring about me the entire afternoon. Each wished to "show" scrolls to me, with the hidden intention of convincing me to buy as many as possible. Word spread like wildfire that a *sahib* (foreigner) was in Naya to seek out scroll paintings. Although these disturbances kept me from catching up on my sleep, it provided me with my first opportunity to see a variety of scrolls and to ask their makers preliminary questions about topics ranging from social issues and political positions to aesthetics and composition techniques. By nightfall of my first day in Naya, I was exhausted and wished only to sleep.

Dozing off early, I was rudely awakened by a loudspeaker blaring an advertisement about an upcoming event that was to take place just outside of the village. I thought I had heard the words "America" and "burning," but then assumed I must have been dreaming terrible things in the aftermath of the events in New York only months before. I didn't give it much more thought that evening, but the next morning after breakfast I went to the tea stalls, where men hang out early in the morning to talk among themselves while smoking and drinking. These are also the places where news from the outside traditionally passes through as people board and alight from buses. Across the street, I spied a flatbed rickshaw with some loudspeakers rigged up on it, and assumed it was the one I had heard the night before. Out of curiosity, I struck up a conversation with the stall's owner who was always up on his local gossip and lore. He told me that a *jatra* (popular theater) troupe would soon be coming to stage a new production and that it would deal with the *durghatana* (accident) in the United States. I recalled those haunting words

Madhusudan Chitrakar showing a scroll in the front room of his house in Naya.

from the night before when I thought I was dreaming: America . . . burning. Just then a young boy came in with a handful of billboards that he was being paid to distribute throughout the Pingla Block in which Naya is situated. What caught my eye was the now familiar image of Osama bin Laden, underneath a headline that read *Amerika Jvalcche* (America Is Burning).

A flatbed rickshaw for hire in Naya used to haul things to and fro. Here the driver is hauling a load of chickens to Balichak.

For the next week, the rickshaw with the loudspeaker cruised frequently through the vicinity night and day and, on the day of the performance, incessantly blared out its message as it moved up and down the main road. Only the number of billboards pasted up throughout the village paralleled the increasing frequency of the loudspeaker. Bin Laden's image, in a white turban and an American army coat, was everywhere. That evening he would be joined by other international personalities, as presidents Bush and Musharraf and Prime Minister Vajpayee would be there on stage with him as well. This was a major event in the village. People from villages all throughout Pingla Block thronged to a fallow rice paddy outside of Naya to watch the grand production staged by an itinerant troupe of actors from Kolkata.

And it was grand! Three enormous stages had been set up, one each to represent the United States and India, and a third shared by Pakistan

Artistic rendering of Osama bin Laden fleeing to Tora Bora by Rabbani Chitrakar in a scroll titled "Laden."

and Afghanistan. I attended the event with Gurupada and a number of other Patuas. At around 8 p.m. we purchased snacks and drinks from the vendors who had set up shop around the perimeter of the massive canopy to house the event, as well as a good supply of *bidi*s, the cheap local cigarettes preferred by the rural masses in India and elsewhere in the subcontinent. Being the only foreigner in a mixed crowd of Hindus and Muslims in the aftermath of 9/11 to be "entertained" by a reenactment of the events made me feel somewhat uncomfortable at first, but as the evening rolled along, we all relaxed and gave in to the spirit of jatra: part reality, part fiction, part soap opera. The spectacle lasted more than five hours without an intermission, and culminated in a sensationalistic crashing of two cardboard airplanes hooked up to wires into cardboard and wood replicas of the Twin Towers, all to the accompaniment of backstage pyrotechnics. On the walk home, I felt melancholy about the reality of the terrorist attacks, but my new Patua friends were excited by the events acted out on stage that night.

The first frame of Manu Chitrakar's painting "Oil Trade Center"
showing the conflagration in New York on September 11, 2001.

A frame from Rahman Chitrakar's scroll titled "Strange Kolkata" in which a rural Patua narrates his first encounter with modernity, here depicted as men sporting Western clothing and contending with traffic. The accompanying song, composed as a first-person narrative by Rahman's father Dukhushyam Chitrakar, begins with "What a strange affair in Kolkata," after which he provides a scathing critique of the loose morals and shady ethics brought about by modernity.

Within a week a number of Patuas, inspired by the jatra performance and storyline, began to produce 9/11 scrolls and accompanying songs. What completely took me aback was how the Patuas could so seamlessly incorporate something so contemporary and juxtapose it with a traditional repertoire that stretches back centuries, if not millennia. This event, and others, raised some questions: First, how does a traditional artisan caste such as the Patua community successfully manage to make the transition

Dukhushyam Chitrakar, master singer and painter, performing for the author in front of his pond.

from a patronage system based on barter to one rooted in a cash economy? Second, to what extent do artisans feel the need or desire to participate in or question modern events and their consequences? Third, what are the implications of a highly localized tradition entering into a dialectical relationship with globalization and transnationalism? These three interrelated themes will be closely explored in this essay.

A panel from Rahman Chitrakar's "Strange Kolkata," depicting his father, Dukhushyam, displaying a scroll to a contemporary audience in Kolkata, after which the men wish to take advantage of him by buying his scrolls at a cheap price and selling them abroad. Dukhushyam sings, "I went to the babus. *They called me to them. 'We'll buy scrolls for a few coins.' They'll sell them abroad! . . . I became immersed in sadness. . . . Oh, I won't be able to get food for my belly, in Kolkata."*

A single framed "Durga" pat by Anwar Chitrakar of the Hindu goddess Durga done in the kalighat *style. On display for sale at a handicrafts fair in Kolkata held in February of 2005.*

AN EVOLVING GENRE

Greater Bengal has been the home of a number of interrelated painting and drawing forms ranging from ritual floor designs known as *alpona* to the modern "traditionalism" of the internationally known and highly acclaimed painter Jamini Roy, whose work reflects the *pat* (scroll painting) genre that is at the center of this essay (University Gallery 1971). In between these two extremes of ritual-based rural forms and urban-based interpretations and developments of rural forms lie a number of other hybrid-painting media, including the urban *kalighat* style developed in Kolkata in the nineteenth century, and the contemporary rickshaw panels so prevalent in Bangladesh.

The power of such popular art forms to address current issues is quite clear. For instance, colonialism is addressed in a scroll called *lal mem-sahib* (red foreign lady) from the independence era, and a *sahib pat* depicting British oppression of Indian freedom fighters (page 25) is still a part of the repertoire of the oldest generation of painters in Naya. But not all is serious on the folk/popular continuum, as is cleverly suggested in the two rickshaw panels of the kung-fu fighting lion and the idyllic village scene

A 1960s replication of a well-known nineteenth-century kalighat *painting depicting a man wrestling with a tiger.*

of animals in the jungle watching television (page 27). Each of these variations provide stark commentaries on their subject matter, as in an image in which we see a scroll painter unraveling a scroll while performing for a rural audience; that is, art about art (page 28).

Cultural and aesthetic change are adequately represented in forms of art that we often naively refer to with such qualifiers as "folk," "traditional," "popular," "outsider," and so on (Shapiro 1989). But, in this essay, I don't focus on definitions but on interpretations of change that hover at the center of such visually expressive traditions. Not only are the Patua scroll painters of Bengal an excellent example of this evolutionary process, but also change is absolutely necessary to the dynamic vitality of the tradition, as the Patuas themselves told me over and over again.

The opening panel of Rani Chitrakar's "Sahib" pat, depicting a freedom fighter being hung from a clock tower by the British for acts of insubordination.

A Bangladeshi rickshaw panel by the artist Naj depicting the invasion of the Pakistani army during Bangladesh's war for independence. The under-clad woman holding the infant represents the "rape" of the nation.

Scroll painter Rani Chitrakar holding her granddaughter, with her daughter Susuma, a budding scroll painter, looking on.

Animals are often used in Bangladeshi rickshaw art to convey a
sense of whimsy but also to skirt the issue of prohibiting human
representation in Islamic art.

An idyllic country scene depicts animals enjoying human comforts—
in this case watching a singing performance on television.

The closing frame of Dukhushyam Chitrakar's "Life Story," in which we see him unraveling a scroll as he sings an accompanying song: "I wrote four or five pat *songs. This time I went to the villages alone . . . But I took rice and coins . . . My mind fell upon scrolls. I had to compose new songs . . . I'd go and sing devotional songs."*

In fact, many say that keeping the repertoire from stagnating goes back to the beginning of the tradition itself. Relating the origin of his lineage, Gurupada concluded with the following statement about the first itinerant Patua:

> ✐ What else shall I say? Perhaps after doing it many times, when after going to a house for the second time, then they would say, "Go away, you've told that story before. This time, if you show us something a little bit different, then everything will be good. Then he got worried. "Its true! What is to be done?" For that reason, he gradually started to compose songs. Then when he started to go to people's houses again, and the villagers would say, "Oh, I see, I see, that picture feller is coming, oh my!" Everyone gathered and said, "Someone give him a place to sit. Will you show us a picture? Everyone is curious." "Yeah, show us, show us, show us!" Then his name became picture feller or Patua feller. After that, when he slowly wrote songs, he used the art of persuading (*patiye*), "Earlier I had told you a story about *patiye*." *Patiye* means persuading with rhyme (*mil*). [here Gurupada breaks into song]:

Manimala Chitrakar singing the song of Satya Pir, a Muslim saint revered by both Hindus and Muslims. Her young daughter assists her here and will one day follow in her mother's footsteps. Most scrolls are unraveled vertically, but "Satya Pir" is one of the few horizontal scrolls.

Listen, listen everyone, listen attentively (diya man).
I have brought out a new pat, *a flood description* (bibaran).

I mean, a rhyme to go along with that word. We say in dialectal Bengali, patiya. *Patiye bala* (speaking in patiya, that is, persuasive rhyme). To rhyme a word with a word, rhyming to make a song. From that the name Patua came to be.

Rhyming *Mahabharata* [one of India's two great ancient epics, the other the *Ramayana*, telling of the great war between the Pandavas and the Kauravas and serving as a repository for many spiritual and moral teachings], writing songs, going from house to house . . . , painting and painting . . . , continuously doing these things, his lineage came about. [In time] the Patuas' fame spread. Slowly, slowly, slowly, slowly, after him, we came. From the *Ramayana* and *Mahabharata* our ancestors—from the reign of the *thakurda*s (ancestors)—they too had sung *Ramayana*, *Mahabharata*, *mangalkavya*s (auspicious poems), *Mangalchandi*. We too have heard the songs from them. Now we sing [them]. ❧

Gurupada then went on to say that as the Patuas moved from village to village attracting new clientele, people started asking for new songs in addition to the mythological ones sung repeatedly by their ancestors. "Your kids are growing up and going to school now," they would say, "argh, reading books, schmucks, looking at newspapers, watching TV!" The audience would ask about how many people died in this or that natural calamity, or why the Babri *masjid* (mosque) was torn down. Then they would suggest that Patuas should compose new songs around such events. They would say, "Yeah, dude, can't you make something really new out of all this?" Gurupada and his colleagues were worried that if they couldn't compose new and interesting material, people would stop patronizing them. He and the others realized that if they weren't able to produce something "mouthwatering," as he put it, the traditional material would no longer be appealing to them. He then concluded by stating the following about how even their children provide information that gets incorporated into the process of composing new songs:

❧ So we also gradually, gradually, gradually started asking how the Ram *mandir* (temple) was broken and how the Babri mosque was ruined. These kinds of things that matter, we take them and write songs about them. And what about that atom bomb that fell on Nagasaki and Hiroshima? The boys and girls, you know, study in college. So they find stuff like Nagasaki and

A frame from Gurupada Chitrakar's scroll called "Atom Bomb" depicting bodies being blown up in Hiroshima. The refrain to the accompanying song goes as follows: "Oh brother, what a strange business in America. Oh brother, what a strange business in America."

Hiroshima in books. Like, how many people were destroyed in 1945 by dropping the bomb. So when the kids study in college, they come home and tell stories to mom and dad. . . . If I take [their story as a] pat, they sing that song along with mom and dad. They say, "Yeah, its true!" If a picture is shown along with it [the song], more enjoyment is aroused. So doing these things, pat has arrived where it is today, and exactly from this [my words] we have the history of pat and its birth. ✺

Gurupada's words show that Patuas understand their artistic tradition in dynamic terms, one that has been in the process of transformation since its inception. While it is true that repertoires are transforming more rapidly today, due to better communication technology, it is quite clear that the Bengali art of painted storytelling was never stagnant, and always involved a certain competence and responsibility on the artist's part to meet the needs and desires of the audience that served, after all, as patrons of the tradition. But as we shall see, as the character of the audience changes, so too does the content of the repertoire.

Svarna Chitrakar singing while taking a break from painting. She works in close association with her brother Manu.

The Patuas, also known as chitrakars (picture makers; hence, their adoption of the term as a surname and caste title), are an indigenous group of Bengalis specializing in the production of painted narrative scrolls (pat) and the performance of songs to accompany their unrolling. The etymology of the term *patua* is unclear, and scholars have been debating its origins for decades. One thing is clear, however. It is related to the word pat. Gurupada Chitrakar told me that the word comes from the Bengali infinitive *patano*, which means to persuade. According to him, the first Patuas had to use rhetoric to lure in, seduce, and persuade their audiences to listen to their songs and pay them for their services.

It is known that the Patuas have been plying their trade since at least the thirteenth century, and most likely for centuries, if not millennia, prior to that (Coomaraswamy 1929; Rao 1995). One camp of scholars claims a post-Aryan origin for this artisan caste, while another—perhaps influenced by nineteenth-century nationalistic-cum-romantic tendencies—suggests a tribal source for the tradition. But who are these formerly itinerant artisans? Myth and oral history combined provide us with some clues. According to the *Brahmavaivartapurana* (Shastri 2004, I.10.16–96), an important Sanskrit text written in Bengal most likely during the thirteenth century, the Patuas were born of a union between Vishvakarma, the celestial architect, and a semidivine dancing girl named Ghritachi, who he then curses to be reborn on earth as a low-caste Shudra (I.10.36–58). While on earth, she gives birth to nine sons (I.10.64), which can be read as nine castes. These nine castes come to be known as the *navasakha* group of the nine recognized artisan castes; among them are the chitrakars. Verse I.10.20 tells us that they are grouped among the lowest three of the nine. This mythological account would suggest that the Patuas were originally Hindu. The text further informs us that this artisan community was cast

Svarna and Manu Chitrakar in the early stages of painting new scrolls.

out of Hindu society because they did not follow canonical procedures in plying their trade. Roughly translated, the critical line (I.10.96) reads, "Chitrakars, for painting pictures untraditionally, have just been expelled [from society] by angry Brahmans." In other words, they did not conform to standards put forth in the *Shilpashastra* (Codes of Art) literature that lay out the aesthetic canons of Hindu iconography. However, other mythological accounts tell a different story of how the group lost their caste status:

    ✒ One day a Chitrakar was painting a scroll of Mahadeva [Shiva] when the deity himself happened to pass by the painter's way. Out of fear, the artist put his brush into his mouth, severely offending the great god. Mahadeva cursed him, saying, "You will hereafter earn your livelihood by painting with polluted brushes. From now on you will be Yavanas [Muslims]!" (Bhattacharjee 1973, 95) ✑

Various legends preserved orally by the group also suggest similar transgressions resulting in loss of caste status and religious affiliation. Take, for example, the following account by a Hindu Patua named Dhirendranath Chitrakar:

    ✒ Long ago our forefathers learned that the Raja [king] was assigning each caste a definite status in society. They decided to approach the ruler for an assignment of status befitting their caste.

The Raja made queries about the nature of their occupation and then asked them to do some modeling and painting to illustrate their point. While painting the deity our ancestors used saliva to moisten the cotton. The Raja happened to observe this highly outrageous act, which infuriated him greatly and he assigned them a very low status in the society. The Patua have since then been unhappy and later they entered into the fold of Islam to elevate their status. They could, however, never give up the traditional occupation that continues to link them to Hindu society. (Siddiqui 1982, 53) ❧

The above legend possibly refers to the reign of Ballal Sen (ca. 1160–78), the second king of the last Hindu dynasty in Bengal who created what has come to be known as the Kulin system, in which he restructured the regional caste system into a rigidly ranked hierarchy of a variety of subcastes. The chitrakars were oppressed as a result of his restructuring, which would explain pragmatically their motivation for converting to Islam when the Sen Dynasty declined and Muslim rulers ascended to power in eastern India.

Shambhu Chitrakar stays home to care for the children, while Svarna travels with her brother to earn a living from painting and singing.

Another account narrated by a Muslim Patua named Pir Bakhsh (also known by the Hindu name Prakash Chitrakar) goes as follows:

❧ Many years ago while our ancestors were Hindus, they were called upon by the Raja named Dakho to make an idol for him. The artists made the image but forgot to put in the *trinayan* [third eye of the deity]. Presuming to have completed the work, they threw the residue of colour in the pond and set forth for their homes, keeping the brushes on their ears. Now it so happened that the Raja noticed the mistake. He sent for the Patuas who were on their way home and called them back to the palace. Having realized their error they sought to rectify it, and since no colour was left, they moistened a *kalam* [pen] with saliva and began putting the third eye on the face of the image. The Raja happened to see this outrageous act and decided to expel them from Hindu society. To the profound grief of the Patua it was decided by the Raja that the offending Patua would be allowed to leave the palace only at very early dawn on the following day, and while going out would accept as their guru the man they first happened to see on their way. Thus the freed Patua happened to see a *mulla* [Muslim cleric] going to give a call (*azan*) for morning prayer. The Patua were thus converted to Islam. (Siddiqui 1982, 53–54). ❧

"The History of the Patuas,"
by Gurupada Chitrakar.

The Patuas of Naya have their own unique story of their origins and how they became painters and singers. Gurupada told it to me on my first visit to his home, and I have heard it many times since from others:

❧ From today, about two-and-a-half to three thousand years ago, there were no Patuas. Pat came exactly at that time, and how it came, that, I'll tell now. There was a big old cave. A demon (*rakshas*) lived in that cave. So when twilight came that demon would come out to wander around and slip into some village. . . . He'd grab a person or two, but before sunrise . . . he would go and slip back into the cave. So, wandering, . . . again and again, village after village, he started to eat people. People from villages near or afar became very worried and used to pass the nights in a state of great fear.... [They traveled] by day, to do farm work, to do business and commerce, but at night remained immersed in a state of great alarm.

So now the demon was euphorically happy that no one could lay a finger on him.... He was so frightening that no one would go near him. He was so incredibly tall, such a big body, very big teeth, fingernails on his hands that he could use in war back then.

Now nuclear weapons have come out but then all that stuff didn't exist. No bombs, cannons, pistols. Now a lot has come out that can destroy from afar. But two-and-a-half to three thousand years ago this kind of stuff didn't exist. In those days you'd probably have a two-hand, three-hand, or four-hand spanned bamboo staff... or a sword about two hand spans long. Approaching the demon with a two-hand or three-hand spanned thing is quite a thing! Perhaps he'd go and fight them, and if he'd catch them, he'd eat them up.

The demon likes eating people.

In this way, he used to eat, and eat, and eat, until one character in a village thought "It's true that if this demon isn't quelled then he'll eat up all the people." People came home at night for a little peaceful sleep or perhaps no sleep at all, [they said] we have to come up with something. We have to devise a plan by which the demon can be destroyed. So each and every person was thinking, thinking how and in what manner to subdue the monster. One wise man came forth and presented a way that the demon might be able to be destroyed.

The clever one sets up the mirror.

He said, "Look, for this demon who interrupts our sleep all night, all of us, nearby or far away, to kill this demon, I have made arrangements." So all the villages' people were happy: "If the demon can be killed by some means, then maybe we will be able to sleep in peace. So tell us, tell us!" ... "Whatever you say, we'll do." [He] said that they should build a glass, like a mirror, as tall as the demon. Perhaps eight foot or ten foot long in height. Perhaps you'll even have to make it a few feet taller than the demon. So they made the mirror really big.

Building it, they took it to that demon's cave, that night, . . . they set up the glass on that road . . . on the day of prayer. At twilight the demon set out from the cave. Seeing it on the road, he went and stood in front of the glass. The light, that blazing light, in the light of the moon, more or less looked great. That demon's image could be seen in the glass. So then the demon became perplexed. "What's the deal? In this cave besides me, there is no other. Where was there a demon larger than me? Huh?" Grimacing, he said, "I have to kill him. If I don't kill him, at some time he might be able to harm me." . . . He boxed that image in the glass.

The demon fights his reflections in the glass fragments.

Ah, now he picks up a big stone, and that one also picks up a big stone. I mean his own image, though. It was a huge boulder. It would have been about two tons heavy. "Picking up a huge stone like this, I'll kill him." Then, he maddeningly throws a forceful pitch at the glass, the demon. The mirror breaks into pieces and pieces. It's glass, you see. It was scattered in the four directions. Tiny, tiny, tiny, tiny fragments and fragments. Many fragments resulted, 220 fragments, then 220 images! A destructive affair! [The demon said], "I saw one. Now because I killed one, it became 200. By what means will I do battle with 200?"

That poor bastard! Surrounding him was the four-directional demon. I mean the mirror fragments. Whatever direction he turned, the image could be seen. He thought, "It's enclosing me, and there's no way to save myself." In that desolate mountain cave, among the stones, bashing in his own head, he died. The next morning, . . . [there was] a meeting. The clever one said, "Let's go. Morning has passed, and it's midday. Let's go see what the glass's condition is." Going there, they saw truly the fragments of glass scattered due to the demon's death. It was a bloody affair! The demon had died. [The villagers said to the clever one], "Wow, it's true you are a divine person! We have to praise you. Now we can work hard all day, come and go as we please, and sleep nicely at night."

One or two people said, "Look, twenty-five or fifty people have come to this meeting. So only we know that the demon has been killed. Only we are relaxed. Thousands and thousands of villagers [who don't know] won't sleep comfortably. How shall we convey the news to them?" Then that clever one said, "You all, one by one, have to go disseminate the state of affairs. . . . It's a question of going and giving. Since you'll be going around from village to village to say these things, [people should] give you some fees." Then, on a canvas, he drew the demon's picture. [Each person made a] drawing and wandered from village to village to describe the event, saying there was no more fear. Saying, "Going and working hard all day, you will be able to rest comfortably in the evening." Why?

"Well, we killed the demon." "Well, how did you kill him?" Filling up that canvas, and showing it over and over and over and over again they established a profession. A caste came to be. Those poor bastards abandoned work. It fell upon them to wander daily in the heat of the sun, through rain, lots of inconvenience. And they wandered from home to home in the wind—the heat of the sun beating down—and life going on. Somehow or the other there was no want. So that's sort of the life.

Showing that picture once, showing it twice, someone would give rice and some change, then view the picture. Some saw it once, twice. If they saw it a third time, they would say, "How far, who is that demon, how many days ago did he get slain?" "OK, come, stay, we'll give you some money, mister. Take it and go. We won't even look at the picture. We know that story. If you prepare something new and come, then we'll look, become happy, and we'll be able to give you something more." In this way, after having gone to every house time after time bringing the news [the people] realized that, "True! We need to do something new. Indeed, the demon died long ago." So gradually [a bard] began to write something new from the *Ramayana* and the *Mahabharata*. Writing those, he started painting pictures to show, too.

The clever one going from village to village to inform people that the demon is no more.

The villagers became very happy and said, "Wow, its true, the *Ramayana* and *Mahabharata*'s war of Rama with Ravana, this abduction of Sita, yes, all this stuff, we've heard. But this picture you have painted and shown, this is a very good thing." Becoming happy, they gave him something. Going on doing this, he assumed an occupation and a livelihood. In those days a villager's life went this way. ❧

In this interesting variation on a theme, the Patuas are not described as victims of either divine curses or royal tyranny. On the contrary, they are heroes empowered by their defeat of the monstrous demon. These narratives, and other variants of them, would make an interesting study in and of themselves, given their structural and thematic similarities. But here I wish simply to draw attention to the fact that both mythological and historical stories suggest an ambiguous social status for the Patuas. They are, in a sense, betwixt and between two realms; or, to be more accurate, two religious worlds: Muslim and Hindu.

What seems to be the case from their occasional mention in various sources ranging from Hindu *puranas* (mythological texts), such as the one cited earlier, to Buddhist story literature (Kapstein 1995), to Islamic historiography is that the Patuas oscillated back and forth from Hinduism and Buddhism to Islam in their perpetual quest for equity and patronage (Bhattacharjee 1980, 1–10). Even though there are still some Hindu Patuas in Bengal, many finally turned to Islam for ultimate solace. These conversions were not philosophical choices so much as they were economic necessities, since Patua survival has always depended on generous patrons. This view corroborates one Bengali skeptic's claim that the Patuas "pay little attention to the doctrinaire aspects of their ever-changing religious faiths, which they embrace to save their skins more than their souls" (Chakraborty 1973, 88). After all, converting to Islam had its benefits, since then the *jizya* tax incumbent upon all "heathens" (i.e., people outside of the Abrahamic traditions) would not have to be paid. Moreover, converting to Islam when the Hindu Marathas (a tribal confederacy) encroached upon eastern India from the west also provided Patuas the military protection of the Muslim Navabs (rulers).

Similar to the mystical Baul singers of greater Bengal, who are perceived to be neither Hindu nor Muslim, the Patuas straddle the ideological border between the two faiths. This is apparent both in name and practice. In rural areas of south Bengal Hindu Patuas often take the artisan surname Pal (as the Kalighat Patuas do) or retain the Chitrakar title, while Muslim Patuas adhere to names common to their faith or use the term Chitrakar or Patua as a surname (Bhattacharjee 1973, 99). In Naya, for example, many Patuas have two names, one Hindu and one Muslim, which allows them to move seamlessly in and out of the two faith communities. Many follow Muslim customs such as male circumcision, funerary rights (e.g., burial as opposed to cremation), and divorce (*talak*), but also follow Bengali Hindu marriage customs such as *gayer halud puja* (turmeric massage ceremony), even though an Islamic religious practitioner performs the actual wedding. To confuse matters even more, the artistic repertoire of the Patuas covers

Hindu topics pertaining to both sacred (e.g., stories from religious lore) and secular themes (e.g., heroes, political events, social strife, natural calamities, etc.). But they also sing the praises of Muslim saints, such as Satya Pir and Gazi Pir.

So are the Patuas Hindu or Muslim? Prior to the partition of Bengal by the British, there did not seem to be any strict sectarian demarcation, yet as religious communalism became a mounting problem, the lines of identity and practice were gradually drawn. Shortly after India's independence, the Hindu Mahasabha (a Hindu nationalist organization) made a concentrated effort to reconvert Muslim Patuas to Hinduism with the *shuddhi* (purification) rite, especially in urban areas such as Kolkata. Later on, the *Bangiya Chitrakar Unnayan Samiti* (Bengali Chitrakar Progress Society) was founded to get the newly reconverted community on the "scheduled caste" register. The struggle is not completely over, however, for official organizations such as these have led to stronger divisions between Hindu and Muslim Patuas in urban areas. Many rural Patuas who still remain do not emphasize such distinctions, and they even attempt to alleviate Hindu/Muslim communal tension through their artistic compositions.

Satya Pir mounted on his tiger in the opening frame of Mantu Chitrakar's "Satya Pir" scroll, which explains why the saint should be revered. Hindus also worship him under the name Satyanarayan. As the accompanying song states, "For Hindus he is Narayan, for Muslims Pir."

Let me provide a wonderful example of what I mean. Communal violence has been an ongoing problem in India, and many thousands of people have lost their lives to it over the years (Larson 1995). The incident that has drawn the most attention is the contentious Babri Masjid affair that led to the razing of a medieval mosque in the town of Ayodhya by extremist Hindus who believed a temple dedicated to Rama once existed where the mosque stood for centuries. The aftermath of the event left many Hindus and Muslims dead, and tempers still run high over this issue. Patuas in Naya sing about this event, but call for constraint and tolerance. The song version of Babri Masjid I present here is once again by Gurupada Chitrakar and the images are from his younger brother Mantu:

"BABRI MASJID"
Scroll by Mantu Chitrakar, song by Gurupada Chitrakar.

We are the human race, one mother's offspring.

We are the human race, one mother's offspring.

Some of us became Hindus.

Again, some became Muslims.

One mother's offspring.

Adam's wife became pregnant.

Sabil and Kabil took birth.

Sabil and Kabil took birth.

Those two brothers took two religions.

Those two brothers took two religions.

Look, look, there is proof in the scriptures.

One mother's offspring.

We are the human race, one mother's offspring.

Marang Burung, say the Santals.

And again the Christians say, they say God.

And again the Christians say, they say God.

Again, those Muslims say Allah.

Again, those Muslims say Allah.

Hindus say Bhagvan.

One mother's offspring.

We are the human race, one mother's offspring.

Usurping religion politics wanders from place to place.

Abandoning all that, sir, everyone live in harmony.

Abandoning all that, sir, everyone live in harmony.

In the name of religion, fighting and killing place after place.

Abandoning all that, sir, everyone live in harmony.

That which is God (ishvar), is nature (prakriti) itself.

Today, though, science is giving proof.

One mother's offspring.

We are the human race, one mother's offspring.

Hindus and Muslims we're all brothers, brothers.

But aside from human nature there is no other actual religion.

But aside from human nature there is no other actual religion.

How could we fight with these brothers, brothers.

We, that is, how could we fight with these brothers, brothers.

We are the human race, one mother's offspring.

That's why, everyone get together and worry.

Destroy this animosity encompassing castes.

That's why we should all get together and move forward.

Destroy this caste animosity.

Let's go, we'll all say it together.

We'll all say the slogan.

One mother's offspring.

We are the human race, one mother's offspring.

A stick-fighting display being performed to the accompaniment of drumming on Naya's main road during the Muslim ritual of Muharram.

After he sang me this song, while displaying his scroll, Gurupada and I talked about the question of religion, and he excitedly said:

↶· These very Patuas, this Hindu-Muslim business, this is, actually very complicated. Patuas, however, from the beginning, were first Hindu. They painted and sang songs, everything according to the Hindu *shastra*s (law books). All Patuas were Hindu. During the Navab [Muslim] rule, 300 or 350 years ago, the Patua lineage, though, was a very small minority community and poverty stricken. And under the Navab's rule, due to the Navab's command, low and naughty people too became Muslims. But in the territory of India there weren't any Muslims. In the territory of India there were perhaps ten families of Muslims. I mean those who were "original" Muslims. Ten families! But in contemporary India now there are perhaps 200 million Muslim residents. But, but, they became Muslims during that Navab's rule. Through his decree, they became Muslims. From that side Patuas also became Muslims. But again, the Patuas became Hindu. Like, we got it from our dads and grandfathers who, suffering from many oppressions, became Muslims, and we too are that religion, we reside in Islam. But again, in the past twenty or twenty-five years some Patuas became Hindus and Kalighat Patuas. They're Hindus. Now they're all Hindus, or Purulia's Patuas, Santal Patuas, they're Hindu. Bankura's Santal Patuas are Hindu, Bihar's Santal Patuas are Hindu. Those that are from the Ramakrishna Mission, they, I mean if you open up history and look, Patuas were all Hindus. But in that Navab's reign, they were all converted. But those in the Ramakrishna Mission took it upon themselves to make them Hindu again. Under the influence of the Ramakrishna Mission, a lot of people went back to being Hindu. So now, perhaps back then we didn't know that our dads and grandfathers were like this. They thought that those distant bastards were Hindu. The Navabs made them Muslims and the Ramakrishna Mission people came and said, "Hey, dude, you have to become a Hindu." Again, someone comes and says, "You have to become a Muslim, dude!" Again someone comes and says, "You have to become a Christian." Alright already, dude, OK, everything's OK. And those Hindus and Muslims they just talk, but for us it isn't necessary. Let there be Hindus, let there be Muslims, all are humans. The fruit of that is, though, that Patuas are Hindu, Muslim, Vaidya, Christian, or etcetera. We scorn no one and remain in harmony with everyone. This is the deal with Patuas and Hindus and Muslims. ❧

Gurupada's historical understanding of his caste's conversion trajectory is, perhaps, limited, but his interpretation sheds interesting light on the community's religious leanings by placing them squarely in-between the two sectarian groups among whom they must live and from whom they continue to seek patronage. Moreover, his explanation also draws attention to the important fact that a variety of proselytizing forces were constantly attempting to sway the Patuas in one religious direction or the other. In the next section, we shall see that this imagery of "in-between-ness" also manifests itself in the spatial layout of the village in which they live.

Naya and Its Environs

Naya *is situated* in the Pingla Block (*thana*) of Medinipur District, which lies south of Kolkata. Medinipur has a long and checkered history, since it has been a hotbed of revolt and unrest for centuries. Historically, it was inhabited largely by the most oppressed and dispossessed tribes and castes of the region, including the ancestors of the present-day Patuas. In the medieval period prior to British rule, arable lands were controlled by "jungle *zamindars*," landlords who referred to themselves as rajas (kings). Under the British these tracts of land came to be known as jungle *mahal*s. The jungle mahals were home to nomadic tribes that lived off the spoils of the land (among them were the Bediyas, a subcaste of the Patuas). Later, as the British East India Company appropriated more and more land, these tribal tenants joined the zamindars to rebel periodically against the British.

A view of the rice fields that engulf the village from Naya's periphery.

Patua dwellings along Naya's main road.

The September 27 Treaty of 1760 between the Muslim Navab, Mire Qasim, and the East India Company put Medinipur under British rule, which allowed them to collect taxes there. Maratha Hindu invasions from the west and a famine in 1770 caused large-scale unrest, but the area was constantly disturbed because, as can be seen on the map included in this volume, it was a border zone harassed by predatory tribes, invasions, levies by other rajas, aboriginal raids, and forced exactions by armed religious mendicants.

As late as 1800, Medinipur was still two-thirds jungle. The tenants of the jungle mahals were either tribal or low-caste Hindus who held land by feudal tenure, but they would quickly give up the plow for the club to exact revenue for the zamindar to whom they were loyal. As the British gradually dispossessed the zamindars of lands, they refused to pay increased revenues and rebelled. The British eventually won out but were never able to restore normalcy in revenue collection, which meant that development was slow, and the area remained primarily agricultural. As the British consolidated power in the region between 1782 and 1807, they gradually managed to take control away from the zamindars through a reformed land revenue system that forced the zamindars to lease their land to others in lieu of heavy annual revenue, resulting in the landlords becoming mere political pensioners.

The decline of the *zamindari* system gave birth to a new class of rural gentry who took the place of the zamindars, and the British Permanent Settlement scheme handed over the vast estates to these middlemen who paid the zamindars modest pensions. Now essentially powerless, the zamindars could no longer protect their peasantry, which led to fragmentation and increasingly shifting loyalties among the laborers. The former zamindari estates were thus divided into *patni*s (lots) of various sizes, each of which was controlled by a middleman called a *patnidar*. The area where Naya and its surrounding land now sit in Pingla (see map) was one such patni in the past, inhabited largely by landless low-caste peasants who were dispossessed permanently of their feudal land claims.

From 1793 to 1853, due to the promulgation of the Permanent Settlement System, Medinipur was primarily agrarian and dominated by a landed aristocracy. This slowly started changing after the introduction of the railroad, which allowed for news to travel more rapidly to the hinterlands. Thus, from 1853 onward to independence in 1947 the influence of modernity creeps in and nationalism slowly takes root, causing more rebellion. However, this was kept in check by the emerging middle class of *bhadralok* (gentlemen), Bengali anglophiles of the nineteenth century who

performed British civil service work. But as supply won out over demand these bhadralok became a disillusioned middle class who had a good knowledge of government and could implant the political consciousness in the peasantry that was needed to oust the British (Chatterjee 1986).

Patuas often aided the aim of independence by painting scrolls and singing songs dealing with British oppression, such as the sahib pat presented in an earlier section and the one presented above. Even after independence, the area continued to be largely rural and agrarian, remaining heavily politicized. In fact, in the 1970s, the area was a haven for the radically violent Naxalite movement, which was brutally put down by the Communist Party of Bengal in the same manner that the British attempted to eradicate Bengali freedom fighters during the preindependence period (Ray 1988).

A scene from Dukhushyam Chitrakar's "Sahib" pat showing a confrontation between a British officer, riding the white horse on the left, and a local insurgent, riding the brown horse on the right.

Today, Medinipur District is the second largest and second most populous in the province, and it is the third most populous district in all of India (Ray 1963, 1:3). It covers over 5,258 square miles, and has over 11,754 villages (according to the 1991 census), the largest number in the province (Dutta 1991). The population in the 1990s was over 8,331,900, with more than 90 percent residing in rural areas. The decennial growth rate over the past forty years has been roughly 23 percent, while the literacy rate in the district is nearing 70 percent, with literacy rates of over 81 percent for males and 56 percent for females (Ghose 1973; Dutta 1991). That the district is economically depressed is attested by the incredible 64 percent unemployment rate (Dutta 1991, vii–viii). Pingla Block has a population of nearly 150,000 (as of 1991), with over 53,000 literate men and slightly over 33,000 literate women. Of Pingla's total population, 26,260 people belong to the

The backside of Naya, surrounded by rice paddies.

so-called Scheduled Castes and Tribes (Dutta 1991, 810–11). The Patuas would be categorized under this ambiguous rubric as "backward."

Naya is a relatively new village on the landscape, and it is one of many that the visitor sees dotting the rural rice fields of Medinipur as one moves deeper into the interior of the hinterland. According to Shyamsunder Chitrakar, who was among the first Patuas to settle here, the village was still in the process of forming when he arrived as a young man. Both he and Dukhushyam Chitrakar settled in around the same time and managed to secure small parcels of land to supplement their respective incomes generated from painting and singing. Dukhushyam is considered to be the Patua *guru* or teacher from whom the current generation of scroll painters learned their craft. Their presence and financial assistance then allowed for chain migration to occur as other related families of Patuas moved to the village from different areas of Medinipur. Today there are thirty-nine

*Shyamsunder Chitrakar sitting in his doorway instructing
his daughter in the art of scroll painting.*

The central entrance into the patuapara from Naya's main road.

Patua families living in a cluster of houses in a self-contained hamlet known as *patuapara* (Patua neighborhood) within the village. Although not all Patua households rely on painting and singing as their main source of income, many do, and currently women as well as men are economically engaged in the production and dissemination of their collective art form. Others who have abandoned the community's traditional craft work as agricultural laborers or rickshaw drivers. Although they are an economically depressed community, even by rural Indian standards, their traditional caste occupation thrives today for reasons that I will explore later in this essay.

Naya covers 844 acres and houses over 447 families. According to the 1991 census, the total population of the village was 2,438, with 138 literate men and 84 literate women, which is a relatively low rate compared to the district's standards. Unemployment is also a problem, with 619 men and 900 women unemployed (Dutta 1991, 814–15), which is the root cause of the high illiteracy rate. As many people told me during my fieldwork, the cost of sending children to school often forces parents to withdraw them, especially girls, who are still being married off at relatively young ages (e.g., fifteen) merely out of economic necessity. This notwithstanding,

the population has been increasing steadily along the same pattern as the rest of the district, moving from 489 in 1951 to its present number. Of this number, my own census of the patuapara in 2002 provided a count of 224 individuals, making it one of the largest hamlets of Patuas in the district, which has the greatest number of Patuas in comparison to the other districts of West Bengal. Virtually every Patua household has at least one family member involved in the traditional caste occupation, and nowadays many have both parents engaged in the business. The latter fact holds mostly true for the current generation, for in the past women primarily made clay dolls (*putul*s) to sell at festivals and ritual occasions. However, under Dukhushyam's guidance many women in their twenties and thirties became involved in their teens and are currently engaged in either painting or singing activities. Another impetus for women's active involvement in the tradition has been external, an issue to which I will return when I discuss repertoires in a later section.

The patuapara inhabits a unique place in the village, in that it straddles a predominantly Hindu population residing on one side of the main road and a predominantly Muslim population on the other. As such, it is neither fully integrated into the Muslim nor Hindu sectors of the

An interior scene of Naya's patuapara.

village. In a sense, it inhabits a point in-between, allowing its residents fluid access to both communities, since the Patuas seek patronage from both Hindus and Muslims. But like their mixed identities, which have to be constantly negotiated in the course of social interaction, their lived spaces also need to be negotiated. Although in terms of caste status, they remain marginal, their physical presence is actually at the center, where Muslim and Hindu culture flows freely back and forth to influence their ideas about the world as well as the content of their painting and singing compositions.

As is true in the rest of Pingla, where in 1961, the last time that secularism was enumerated, there were 66,575 Hindus and 5,034 Muslims, Hindus are clearly the majority in the village, as they are in the rest of the district (3,130,645 Hindus; 330,015 Muslims) and the country (Ray 1963, 1:iii–iv). But although many Patuas claim formal allegiance to Islam or Hinduism (and even a few to Christianity) in theory, in practice most are fond of the saying "*na hindu, na musalman*" (neither Hindu nor Muslim), and they constantly call for tolerance and compassion, as we saw with the Babri Masjid song and scroll earlier. In fact, the creed of the Patua included at the beginning of this volume makes this point quite clearly as well. However, due to increasing pressure on all sides, Patuas must continually engage in what we might call image management to stay in favor with both communities.

A row of homes in the interior of the patuapara. Those who can afford it replace the thatched roof with a tin one, which requires less repair.

One of the consequences of performing the delicate task of identity negotiation for cultural and economic purposes has been ongoing marginalization and constant impoverishment. Many Patua families in Naya live in abject poverty in small mud huts on the roadside without indoor plumbing and, in some cases, no electricity. Yet a few others in the interior of the patuapara are more fortunate and have some basic essentials like their own tube wells, outhouses, indoor electricity, and, in two cases, indoor toilets. By and large, however, the Patua community's economic standards are far lower than those of other people in the village. Large landowners, for example, live in two- and three-story concrete houses with all the amenities, including ceiling fans, telephone, and television, while others have neatly groomed and well-kept traditional waddle and thatch houses. Yet there are still others who live at the same level of poverty as the Patuas do, which is not surprising, given the high rate of unemployment.

A finer house in the traditional Bengali style with a well-landscaped garden.

An affluent two-story Hindu home in Naya.

A fancy modern house, located along Naya's main road, owned by a Hindu landlord.

The closing two frames of Rani Chitrakar's scroll titled "Literacy."
The top frame shows Saraswati, the Hindu goddess of learning. The
closing frame shows women and a man in a classroom with slates in
their hands learning how to read Bengali.

A day laborer digs a path-side television cable ditch with an adze.

Even though up until a few years ago phone service was rare and unreliable, today many people in Naya use cell phones, own VCRs and DVDs, have cable hookup for their televisions, or use satellite dishes. And in February of 2004 ditches were being dug to have all of these services available to those living in the interior, away from the main road along which the electricity, phone, and cable lines run. Now, even those in remote interior areas of the village will have access to many of the amenities available to those along the main road and in the towns. In this regard, the Patuas are most fortunate, since some of the wealthier ones who live at the front of the para are close enough to the road to avail themselves of such amenities, if they can afford it. Despite the fact that development in Medinipur has been slow at best, Naya is gradually starting to reap the benefits, which in turn has opened up new possibilities for the Patuas.

A farmstead in the interior of Naya village that will soon have access to cable.

All of these factors—economic development, more efficient modes of communication, greater access to material goods, limited literacy, and ongoing religious and social negotiations—have been playing an important role in the artistic productions of the Patua community.

THE SCROLLS: Types, Technique, and Style

*G*enerally *speaking, three types of pats exist*: (1) *jarano* (rolled), (2) *chaukosh* (square or rectangular), and (3) kalighat (which refers to the distinctive style that emerged from the footpaths of Kolkata's famed Kalighat temple in the nineteenth century). To this list must also be added the tribal *jadu* (magic) pats—also known as *chakshudan* (gift of eyes) of the Santal Parganas, which are really a separate topic and beyond the scope of this brief essay (but see Hadders 2001).

Some scholars believe that the scroll paintings were originally done on jute fiber cloth that was given a smooth finish with a thin layer of fine clay paste mixed with cow dung and water (Chakraborty 1973, 84). When this mixture dried on the cloth it was rubbed smooth so as to provide an even and solid surface for the artist's brush. The preparatory process would then be followed by covering the surface with a moist layer of chalk dust mixed with rice glue. Also in the past, successive layers of paper were stuck together with rice glue and rolled flat to serve as canvases, but today some Patuas paint primarily on recycled, whitewashed paper, which is sewn together and then reinforced on the back side with a thin cotton cloth, such as discarded *sari* material, in order to give the creation durability and pliability. In contrast, the rectangular pats, probably best known from the Oriya tradition to the south of West Bengal (Mohanty 1984), are painted on a wider variety of materials, and influenced the gradual production and evolution of the so-called kalighat style that flourished in the nineteenth and early twentieth centuries (Jain 1999). In Naya, however, virtually everyone now uses commercial poster paper that is stocked in one of the village shops.

A frame from a Santal pat *depicting* "The Creation of the Universe."

Sheets of poster paper being sewn together to create a canvas.

Gurupada Chitrakar rolling a sewn, blank canvas to mold it into shape.

The first step in creating a canvas is sewing sheets of poster paper together. After all of the sheets are sewn together, the canvas is rolled up several times to mold it into its proper shape. The images are then sometimes outlined on the canvas with lampblack or vermilion paste, but most of Naya's Patuas simply use a pencil. Next, the individual frames are demarcated by outlining the borders. Each frame corresponds to the size of one sheet of poster paper, so that the borders cover up the thread lines connecting the frames.

Primary colors—white, yellow, black, red, blue, and green—are then used to complete the field with broad, bold brush strokes. Occasionally, but rare these days, gold leaf and silver leaf are delicately added to the final product. Traditionally, these mineral- and plant-based colors would be ground and added to a paste prepared by boiling barley or the seeds of the tamarind tree. But in Naya, the viscous sap of the wood apple tree (*bel*) is used as a binder, to which water is added as necessary to obtain the desired consistency. Most of the materials needed to prepare paints are grown locally or available in the market, such as turmeric root for yellow, broad bean leaves for green, pomegranate juice for red, lime for white, and indigo for blue. Black is either made from lampblack or from burnt rice that is ground into a fine black powder. By mixing these together in various combinations to achieve the proper hue, other colors are created. Some Patuas, however, forego this laborious process and use commercial paints, especially when they are using alternative types of canvases, such as cloth. Even so, a number of senior Patuas insist that commercial paints are inferior, cracking and fading over time. Moreover, they say, bugs will eat the commercial paints but not the natural ones. Both of these are important

Gurupada covering the thread lines of the canvas by painting on a border.

After the borders are demarcated, the field is painted in with a thicker brush prior to the detail work that completes the scroll.

Rukkini Chitrakar, Gurupada's wife, making yellow paint by mixing turmeric powder with water, after which the wood apple sap in the bottle on the left will be added to fix the color.

Nanigopal Chitrakar's "Christ"
pat, *painted on cloth.*

pragmatic concerns since the scrolls are often exposed to harsh weather and used continuously in performance, and when they are stored at home they are shoved between the beams and roofs of the houses, where they are further exposed to insects, rodents, and occasionally snakes who take refuge in the thatch. However, those who now only paint to sell the scrolls do not feel that the type of paint matters. Similarly, commercial brushes made out of synthetic fibers are becoming more prominent, but the older generation of painters with whom I have worked still use squirrel tail brushes for fine lines and billy goat bristles for rougher background work. Once the painting is completed, cloth is glued to the back to provide longevity, after which the completed scroll is placed in the sun to dry.

Paints are often made in advance in coconut shells when the raw materials are in season, then stored in plastic jars for year-round use.

Although these days the rectangular pats are painted primarily for commercial purposes, such as sale to pilgrims and tourists, the scroll paintings were not originally intended for sale. Instead, a Patua would use the finished product as a prop for his singing performances.

Carrying a bag of scrolls over his shoulders, moving around from village to village and house to house, he would solicit his services for whatever modest fee he could get. The first frame of the scroll normally depicted the major character in the story, as the singer would call for the attention of the audience and explain who it was about. Each frame would then unfold the narrative plot as the Patua manipulated the scroll to the pace of his singing. At the conclusion, a closing frame depicting the court of Yama, the king of death, would be shown in order to remind the indi-

Naju Chitrakar gluing cloth from a discarded sari onto the back of a scroll.

Naju and her mother-in-law, Jamuna Chitrakar, carry the completed scroll to a field to dry in the sun.

Shyamsunder Chitrakar approaching a house to offer his services.   *Showing the first frame to attract and entice the audience.*

vidual of the transitory nature of life and to provide a moralistic slant to the narrative, not to mention to scare the audience into providing him with a larger fee. Nowadays, this practice is falling into disuse, even though Yama is still found from time to time in a frame of the painting. Sometimes, a song closes with a threat employing Yama's assistance in torturing the would-be patron if he does not provide a generous gift in exchange for the performance. Along with threats, flattery is also employed to charm the would-be patron into giving more: "Hear me, kind sirs, hear what I say. Get me a piece of cloth from your home. If you give me money or rice, *babu* (sir), you will never suffer. Your fame will spread through the whole world. If you don't give me anything, babu, let me tell you now. The women will eat up all your food and send you out to fend for yourself" (Singh 1998, 114). At any rate, the thematic contents of the Patua repertoire have always been moralistic, covering sacred and secular themes. The famous nineteenth-century Bengali folk art revivalist, Guru Saday Dutt, divided the Patua repertoire into three categories: heroism (e.g., epic narratives), worldliness (i.e., secular), and spiritual quests (Dutt 1990). Although these divisions serve a useful function in ordering the large range of sources utilized by the Patuas, they are not rigid boundaries; even the most sacred stories told by these itinerant performers fulfill an entertainment function, just as other means of rural media (e.g., jatra) in West Bengal do.

As an example, the cult of Gazi Pir that took firm root in the Sunderbans of south Bengal reflects not only the dual Hindu/Muslim background of the Patuas but also the sacred/secular interaction in some of their songs (pages 68-69).

Captivating the audience.

Concluding a song and coming to the end of a scroll.

A frame from a scroll by Pabi Chitrakar about Yama's punishments in one of the netherworlds. This type of scroll is known as "Yama" pat.

*Shahi-Sekander marries King Bali's daughter, the opening
frame of Rahman Chitrakar's "Gazi Pir" pat.*

The name of the Gazi's father is Shahi-Sekander.
He built a house of jewels at Medina.
From the subterranean regions he married the daughter of King Bali,
And from the union was born the pir Zinda (living) Gazi.
Says Gazi to Kalu Rai, "Oh brother of mine!
Let us give up the throne and become fakirs (mendicants)."
So the Zinda Gazi wandered about cities and bazaars as a fakir,
And throughout the land Hindus and Musalmans offered shirni (a special
*   sweet) to him.*

First he went to the house of the goala (milkman).

"Give me some dahi (yogurt) first, Oh Nanda Ghose," said he,

"So that I may partake of it.

Let the best cow of the herd be milked for me."

The foolish daughter of the milkman recognized not the pir.

She had the dahi in her pot but she denied it and so imposed upon the
     Gazi, and lo!

The moment she left the house a tiger came and carried away the best cow
     of the herd.

The white cow of Kalachand also, the tiger took.

The milkman's mother took a lathi (stick) from the door, and beat the
     tiger.

She uttered a yell and hit the tiger on its back.

The tiger carried away her daughter-in-law, seizing her hair with his
     teeth.

Four men sit in a ring, and old Mother Ganga rides on the makara
     (crocodile).

The father coughs and smokes the hookah,

And while the mother blows on it the fire burns his beard.

The old woman beats her son-in-law and dances wildly.

She beats her son-in-law's father and stands in a coquettish way.

When asked to work she feigns fever.

When she gets an offer of marrying again, she runs away.

She does not give away her wealth nor does she spend it on herself,

And so the miserly woman hides her money under a tree before her death.

The mother of Becha goes to catch fish in the Koaranga bil (pond).

While she goes to catch fish the kite carries away her khongpa (hair bun),

And so the unfortunate woman weeps for her khongpa,

And makes up a khongpa with kachu leaves.

With anything she finds handy she ties the khongpa with cane and with
     turmeric powder,

And lo! You can see the veritable city of King Ravana in the midst of her
     khongpa!

Yamaduta and Kaladuta are on the right and left,

While, in the middle sits the mother of King Yama.

She holds a big vessel of copper before her;

On the vessel she places the heads of sinners and boils and eats them.

(adapted from Dutt 1990, 78–79).

This version of the song, collected at the end of the nineteenth century, demonstrates many of the points that I have made so far. The narrative addresses the socioreligious issue of Hindu-Muslim interaction and, finally, uses a secular aside dealing with a mischievous and suggestively promiscuous woman to voice concerns about the moral repercussions that a "fallen one" of this sort might face in the underworld (e.g., getting one's head boiled or genitals mauled). The song deals with sacred and secular issues within the same frame of reference by utilizing comical elements aimed at entertaining the audience while at the same time providing listeners with religious instruction. This formulaic pattern seems to hold true for much of the traditional repertoire of the Patuas. Patuas used to draw heavily on medieval Bengali *mangalkavya*s (auspicious poems) for inspiration to compose their own apocryphal versions. These hefty episodic texts often dealt with religious conflict between competing sects, with the deity being honored in the hymn usually winning out in the end and thus establishing worship. The *Manasamangal*, for example, praises the local goddess of snakes, Manasa, describing her various exploits during her rise in popularity. The particular scroll used here to illustrate is by Gurupada Chitrakar.

Frame 1. Manasa trades insults with Chand Sadagar.

Frame 2. The daughters- in-law paying obeisance.

The most popular depiction of the *Manasamangal* tells the plight of the defiant and stubborn merchant Chand Sadagar. First we see the goddess Manasa trading insults with the wealthy merchant Chand Sadagar, while his wife worships her from the sidelines. Manasa curses him by vowing to kill his six sons. Further, his seventh, unmarried son is to be killed on his wedding night. In the second frame we see Chand Sadagar being paid obeisance by his daughters-in-law, with his wife and seventh son, Lakshmindar, looking on. In the third frame we see the wedding negotiation, where Behula, the bride-to-be, is scrutinized. The fourth frame is divided into two. On its left, the newlywed couple is transported in a palanquin to their nuptial quarter, an iron chamber that is supposed to keep them safe from the goddess's serpentine wrath. All is to no avail,

70

since on the right we see Lakshmindar being bitten and killed by one of Manasa's snakes, that manages to slip into the iron chamber after all.

Next we have another panel to signify the oncoming climax of the narrative. Behula vows to accompany Lakshmindar down the river of death to the realm of Yama in order to appease the goddess. In frame five, Behula bids farewell by touching the feet of her father-in-law, then prepares to sail with her husband's corpse. The next frame is lengthy and multiple actions are occurring simultaneously. We see the major frame surrounded by a number of other actions: the six dead brothers looking on from the side, jackals and crocodiles approaching, attracted by the stench of decaying flesh, and so on. Finally, arriving in *patal* (the underworld), Behula worships all of the gods (including the white-skinned Yama here). Manasa is pleased with her devotions and revives all of the brothers and her husband, who are seen sailing back home together again as an extended family. In the last frame, the three main characters finally worship Manasa together, but the stubborn Chand Sadagar does so reluctantly, as is witnessed by the use of his left hand for worship (Inglis 1979).

The Chand Sadagar episode is a fairly well-known story in Bengal, and the version included here follows the medieval literary source quite closely. A noticeable creative deviation from the medieval *Chandimangal* text is apparent in the Chandi/Durga scroll and song, on page 74, a creative adaptation of the sixteenth-century *Chandimangal* epic poem composed by Mukundaram Chakrabartti, affectionately known as *kavikankan* (jewel of the poets). The Chandi narrative contains two independent story cycles. The first, older one is about Kalketu, who kills animals in the Kalinga forests (of northeastern Orissa) for a living. Chandi is a local forest goddess protecting animals who is worshipped by the Byadha (fowlers and hunters) tribes. She is supplicated by the animals and takes measures to bring Kalketu under control. For some days he can't catch anything in

Frame 3. Behula is scrutinized.

Frame 4. Wedding procession and chamber where Lakshimdar is poisoned.

Frame 5. Behula vows to follow her husband's corpse down the river of death.

Frame 6. Sailing down the river of death to Yama's court.

his net. Finally he catches a lizard and brings it home. The lizard is the goddess in disguise. Kalketu goes in search of his wife, while the lizard becomes a beautiful young girl. Eventually, she reveals herself to Kalketu and bestows riches on him, but he is later attacked by the king of Kalinga and taken prisoner. Chandi once again comes to the rescue and Kalketu is freed. All Kalingans become her devotees.

The second story is somewhat more complex and usual in the genre. A wealthy merchant from Ujani named Dhanapati, who worships Shiva, angers the goddess by breaking her sacred water pot that his wife is worshiping to guarantee him a successful voyage to Sri Lanka. While he is sailing, he spies Kamalakamini, a divine lotus-girl, eating and belching up elephants. He goes to a local king who does not believe him and imprisons Dhanapati. After his father does not return, his son, Srimanta, then goes in search of him and also encounters the elephant-eating lotus-girl. He goes to the king too and says he will show him this incredible sight. The king agrees to go on a wager. If he can produce Kamalakamini, Srimanta can marry his lovely daughter; if not, he will be put to death. Of course, he cannot produce the spectacular vision and is sentenced to death. Just as the execution is about to take place, the goddess Chandi arrives in the guise of a grandmother and begs for her grandson's life. Upon hesitation, she sends her demon army and they defeat the king, forcing him to marry his daughter to Srimanta. In the end, the father, his son, and his new daughter-in-law return home with a wealth of goods and everyone lives happily ever after worshiping Chandi. Such creative adaptations are the hallmark of Patua performance art, and at least one scholar argues that it was precisely for this reason that they were cast out of Hindu society in the *Brahmavaivartapurana* (McCutchieon 1989, 22). Because tradition generally tends to be orthodox, expanding the aesthetic canon of tradition can be risky business. Not surprisingly, it has been an issue that the Patuas have had to contend with for much of their history. Yet even though change and adaptation have been a part of their survival strategy from the beginning, modern circumstances have accelerated the process immensely.

Frame 7. Chand Sadagar finally worships Manasa.

Srimanta encounters Kamalakamini devouring elephants in this frame of Amit Chitrakar's "Chandi/Durga" *pat.*

It should by now be evident that even in the ancient and medieval past, narrative singers with their pictorial props discussed issues pertinent to their contemporary situations. Doing so allowed them to thrive by providing not only religious instruction and entertainment but also local and national news. This can only be rational speculation, however, since sources that mention picture showmen do not provide detailed ethnographic descriptions of their activities (Lüders 1940, 406–414; Varma 1961).

Jumping closer to the present, however, provides us much more detail. In the 1930s, for example, the Patua as newscaster picked up on a sensationalistic tragedy that occurred in the district of Cooch Behar. The story came to be known as "Father Causes Murder by Son." According to accounts, Subal Datta, of Mirzapur, Cooch Behar, caused one of his sons to kill a second son when the plot was actually intended to kill the son-in-law Rashbehari. As the narrative goes, Subal Datta had two sons and a daughter. The daughter, Usharani, was married to Rashbehari who lived in nearby Haripur. Usharani was smart and beautiful, as was Rashbehari. The singer tells us that he passed his IA exam in Bombay, where he worked and diligently sent money home to the family every month. Everything was fine until one day Usha received a letter out of the blue stating that Rashbehari had died in a plane wreck, along with all of the other passengers. Usharani returned to her father's home and was eventually remarried to an old but wealthy zamindar named Balai. Usharani, being *ati sati* (very

74

chaste), never consummated the marriage, and one day news came that Rashbehari was not really dead, since he never got on the plane in the first place. So Usha returned to her father's house. The son-in-law returned to his wife, but the father and his two sons plotted to kill him in order to keep the daughter married to old Balai. Usha found out and informed Rash, who snuck out in the middle of the night. Just then, the two brothers came to the room to murder the son-in-law. Not seeing anyone in the room, the elder brother comes out and is stabbed to death by the younger one, who mistakes him for Rashbehari. A long trial ensues and the father and brother are imprisoned (Sen Gupta 1973, 61–62).

Such historical accounts were reworked, exaggerated, and sensationalized in typical journalistic fashion to keep people interested and listening. Another common theme that hinted at modernistic themes was the illicit love affair or spoiled wife seeking divorce:

> *I won't stay in that house of yours.*
> *Ah, what a pleasant life I have!*
> *You are unable to provide me*
> *with clothes and soap.*
> *Now I'll bid farewell,*
> *[and] I'll wed a new husband.*
> *I'll get spectacles. I'll take shoes.*
> *I'll stay happy with soap.*
>   (retranslated from Sen Gupta 1973, 64)

This poignant verse deals extensively with the issue of modernity. The soap, spectacles, and other accoutrements of British import provide not only the raw material for a scathing critique but also a moralistic argument for returning to the old ways. Needless to say, this wayfaring wife will not have a pleasant time with Yama, and as we have already learned, the British are also critiqued in the Patua repertoire.

Verses such as these alleviated social and religious tension to a certain degree through comical and informative performances, keeping the rural masses entertained and the Patuas fed. But as the introduction of chromolithographs and oleographs flooded the market, the visual dimension of Patua art soon began losing its appeal (Pinney 2004). People still enjoyed hearing their songs, no doubt, but their painting style looked dull in comparison to the brightly colored and affordable prints readily available in markets. The death knell was the introduction of the cinema talkies, accelerating the erosion of the patronage base that has always been the economic backbone and justification for this performance genre. In a tongue-in-cheek fashion, a Patua touches upon this in the following verse:

A scene from Jamuna Chitrakar's scroll about independence called "1947," showing people flocking to the cinema hall to watch movies. She sings, "some go honking in rickshaws, some in motorcars, or by bullock cart."

*Oh my, oh! Such a fever! After the talkie's play came,
the talkie hall's wind opened [the girl's] veil!*

(retranslated from Sen Gupta 1973, 60)

From one perspective, the pleasures of modernity bring about the evils of sensuality and other vices endemic to our age. It is always difficult to interpret the Patua's coding, however, since we have to keep in mind that he sings for his bread. Therefore, to stay fed, he must compose with the patron in mind. Since the patron was often a village headman or wealthy landowner with orthodox leanings in the past, it served the Patua well to take a less than liberal attitude. But occasionally, he would speak his mind, as in a verse complaining that it is a great pity and mental agony that babus still control rations after independence of the nation. So the Patua was clever, manipulating and composing verses according to the likes and dislikes of his patron. Yet once in a great while, he would cry out against the established system of social and political injustices.

The scroll narratives also have different meanings to different people. For example, gender makes a difference in how a song is understood. Male Patuas in Naya interpret the retranslated text (on page 75) as being about women who become too westernized and lose the homely qualities

characteristic of a good Bengali housewife. Yet once, when the men were away at a political rally, I found myself sitting in the courtyard of Jamuna Chitrakar's home, looking at scrolls. Excited that she had one on the theme of 1947, I asked her to sing it for me, which attracted a crowd of other women to watch me recording the old woman. The women giggled throughout her rendition of the song. After Jamuna finished, I asked the crowd why they were laughing so much. I received a variety of opinions that seemed almost "feminist" in the Western sense of the term. All who spoke did not see this song as about a fallen woman at all. To the contrary, they interpreted it as a woman empowering herself by not accepting uncritically the barking of her husband. "You see," one grandmother told me, "we can demand things from our husbands, and if they don't cough it up, we can split!" Just then the bicycle bells of the men entering the para could be heard, and the women quickly dispersed to return to their domestic chores. Perhaps female empowerment is still only a desire for Patua women, since there are many paradoxes in Patua theory and practice, as we'll see in the next section. Nonetheless, the very fact that women explained the narrative to me in a subversive way suggests that they are already walking down the road of liberation.

Jamuna Chitrakar showing the author an unfinished scroll in 2005.

MODERN LIFE AND CHANGE

What is most striking about the Patuas is their incredible resilience, their ability to adapt their art form to modern exigencies by addressing issues of current interest. It is no wonder, then, that they have survived to some degree, even though many Patuas have been forced into other occupations. Many urban Patuas sing no more, but they do continue to work with their hands as wall painters, image-makers, signboard painters, and so on (Siddiqui 1982). Those who continue to perform the hereditary occupation of the caste, as many in Naya indeed do, find themselves sitting on the concrete sidewalks of Kolkata, in lobbies of five-star hotels, and at crafts fairs all around India and even abroad selling scrolls rather than singing about them. In other words, as traditional patronage has declined, Patuas have had to explore new venues and entice new audiences. To be successful at this, they also continue to compose about new themes.

Scroll paintings on display for sale at the annual West Bengal Handicrafts Fair held in Kolkata in early spring 2005.

Patuas come from all over the province to the handicrafts fair and camp there for the two-week duration. Because of commodification, competition has become fierce, and many artists complain that only foreigners buy the scrolls these days.

In addition to performing the more traditional themes coming from their dual Hindu/Muslim religious heritage, Patuas now find themselves painting and singing more and more about famine and flood relief, elections, birth control, ecological awareness, AIDS, 9/11, and, most recently, the tsunami that devastated a portion of the southeastern coast of peninsular India.

It is no understatement to say that modernity has resulted in a substantial loss of traditional patronage from rural audiences, which means that the Patuas must now seek out new ways to market their craft (Hauser 1994, 2002). The most noticeable change is that instead of using the scrolls as a prop for the performance of the tune, Patuas are now selling the scrolls. In other words, no longer are the song performances central to the

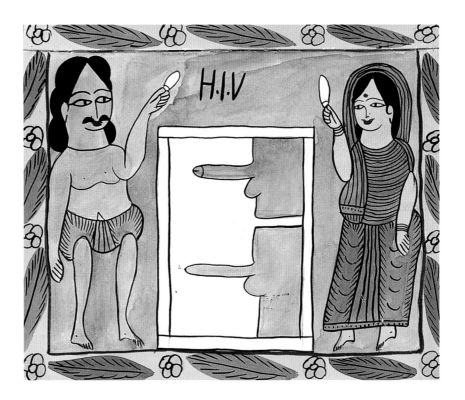

A frame from Rani Chitrakar's "AIDS" *scroll advocating condom use.*

economic dimension of the tradition, and some painters do not even bother composing new songs, just new scrolls. One Patua in Naya said, "Foreigners don't understand Bengali anyway, so why bother. They just want the pat." Patuas with this sort of attitude are now mass-producing scrolls for popular consumption. Some, such as Gurupada, Manu, Svarna, and Rani do continue to innovate and compose. Gurupada and Manu even keep notebooks in which they first compose their songs. After completing the verses, they paint the accompanying scroll. Svarna and Rani, in contrast, being virtually illiterate, compose in their heads, or have a literate male relative write it down. But since they cannot read, it does them little

good to have a new song on paper. In all of the cases, whether oral or written, a narrative is first constructed, after which it is committed to canvas. Many Bengali intellectuals believe that the tradition is waning as a result and will not survive another generation (e.g., McCutchion 1989). But is this really the case? I do not believe that it is.

Much recent ethnographic literature on material culture has focused on the effect that globalization and transnationalism (Appadurai 1996) have had on the production and consumption of traditional arts (e.g., Marcus and Myers 1995; Steiner 1994). By and large, these studies indicate that traditional art forms are subject to mass production and commodification when they are excised from local contexts for the purposes of international trade and display. The results of such "traffic in culture" vary from place to place, but one thing generally found to be true by investigators is that the local production of art becomes competitive and contested when it enters the international arena. In the Indian context, Helle Bundgaard's (1996, 1998) studies of Orissa's *patta citra* (leaf picture) tradition provide useful insights into the arenas within which meanings and values are constructed. She moves beyond the local and regional dimensions of the tradition to discuss elite discourses that have occurred on national and international levels ever since official awards were initiated to

Gurupada studying a new song that he composed about the south Indian tsunami of December 2004.

recognize the aesthetic value and artistic merit of the genre. Such a global scenario of competition stimulated by artistic fame and economic potential has led to both cooperation and conflict in Orissa, which has further resulted in ongoing formations of what she refers to as contested art worlds. I see the same kind of thing happening in Naya, where, due to stiff competition, all sorts of conflicts arise within the Patua community over issues of patronage, jealousy, innovation, and even ownership, ever since intellectual property rights became an issue in India (Korom 2006)

The traffic in Indian art is by no means new (Davis 1997), but it has increased considerably in modern times since the Festival of India toured the United States in 1985–1986 (Kurin 1988). Since then, Indian festivals have occurred in many nations of the European Union, as well as in Australia and New Zealand, which has exposed numerous local artists to potentially new audiences and markets. These brief visits in turn have conditioned the way that local artists now cope with modernity in India (e.g., targeting tourists as potential patrons). The Patuas of Naya with whom I have worked are a good case in point because a small number of them have been abroad. Gurupada has visited the United States, Spain, and Italy. Dukhushyam has been to Australia, while Svarna and her brother Manu visited Sweden (Haglund and Malmeström 2003). Rani has been to Scotland. In each instance, they returned home a little wiser and a little wealthier. These trips have inspired them to continue experimenting with their tradition. But it has also inspired jealousy in those less fortunate Patuas who have not received international invitations. Moreover, an increasing number of what we might call "culture brokers," such as members of the West Bengal Crafts Council, are collaborating with Patuas to devise alternative materials on which to paint (e.g., T-shirts, lampshades) and to create new contexts for marketing their tradition (e.g., folk festivals, crafts fairs, and hotels). Inevitably, this has led to commodification, but also more diversity and a certain amount of economic empowerment that has allowed some of Naya's Patuas to renovate and expand their homes, build outhouses, install telephones, and purchase wall clocks, televisions, and DVD players.

Nongovernmental organizations (NGOs) have also collaborated with Patuas to compose songs on themes such as AIDS prevention, dowry deaths, the importance of literacy and education, rural hygiene, tsunami relief, and a variety of other pressing social issues. Yet outsiders are not responsible for initiating all of the new materials in the Patua repertoire. Svarna, to use just one interesting example, created a scroll about the crash of the Titanic after the movie became a hit (Sengupta 2004). Ironically, she did not see the movie herself, but heard the story from someone who did,

People being naughty on the Titanic before its fatal crash, with Leonardo DiCaprio and Kate Winslet secretly coupling at the center and looking at her naked portrait in the upper right. To the left is the dance going on in the ballroom. This is how Svarna Chitrakar interprets the reason for the crash, in her scroll "Titanic." Divine retribution ultimately destroys human folly.

felt moved by it, and decided to compose a song and scroll. After all, as I have been suggesting throughout this essay, Patuas have always been innovative, from their legendary beginnings singing news of the demon's death to decrying the oppression of colonialism and the loose morals resulting from popular Western culture making inroads into Indian society. All of this suggests that it has been both a passion for their craft, as well as a necessity of survival, that has motivated the Patuas to remain current in their thinking.

Some critics of globalization suggest that it leads to homogeneity and a generic global culture based on kitsch and Western pop culture, insisting that the "one-road-to-modernity" model stifles indigenous innovation. This may be true to a certain extent, with Wal-Mart and McDonalds franchises opening throughout the world, but I wish to suggest that there is plenty of room for local creativity where the Patuas are concerned. In fact, the most successful Patuas have been able to negotiate their artistic tradition in modern times the same way that they have been negotiating their identities over the centuries. That is, they allow innovation to creep into their tradition by traditionalizing it. What I mean by "traditionalizing" is taking new elements and casting them in a familiar indigenous mold. Let us take as an example the Ode to 9/11 with which I began this essay. The jatra play that inspired the Patuas' compositions about the New York tragedy did not just simply retell the events as they unfolded, but indigenized it to suit local aesthetic sensibilities (Biswas 2005). Hence the storyline could not just be an objective historical recounting. Instead, a subplot concerning the son of an affluent Bengali family who goes to the United States, engages in excessive carnal activities, and perishes in the World Trade Center inferno is inserted into the actual events that transpired on that fateful day. Moreover, the moral of the story was mythologized to send a religious message that the world is becoming increasingly sinful and must repent. In so doing, the writer of the play intentionally drew on the rural audience's expectations to give them what they wanted. Similarly, the Patuas drew on the theatrical production to create their own painted and sung versions (Mukhopadhyay, In press).

Another graphic example will make the point quite clear. Gurupada paints in a traditional Medinipur style that is epitomized in the Manasa pat discussed earlier in this volume. Some years ago, when the Alliance Française in Kolkata had convened a conference in 1989 to commemorate

Gurupada Chitrakar's depiction of Louis XVI in his "French Revolution" *scroll.*

the bicentenary of the French Revolution, Gurupada was inspired to paint a French Revolution scroll based on the narrative history given to senior scroll painters by French employees of the Alliance Française (Alliance Française 1989). Although the story was new to his repertoire, he painted Louis XVI to look just like Lakshmindar, the youngest son of Chand Sadagar in the Manasa scroll. Even more remarkably, he also painted a scroll about me coming to Naya in which I look like both Louis XVI *and* Lakshmindar. The point here is that the Patuas consciously allow new themes to enter into their collective repertoire to expand the canon, but as new themes enter, they get reworked to suit their own aesthetic sensibilities. That is why a contemporary professor from New England can look like the clone of French royalty or a wealthy medieval Bengali merchant's son. What this suggests to me is not a mimicking of Western trends in the quest to become modern, but rather a kind of alternative modernity that is a subtle mixture of internal and external influences, neither fully indigenous nor fully foreign. And this is how it must be, if the Patuas wish to assert their own agency into the process of marketing themselves and their goods to a globalizing transnational market.

So, in closing, even though one might see many new themes cropping up in the repertoires of the Patuas, some still dogmatically tell the old stories that have been popular for centuries. The singer, however, often recontextualizes these by using interpretive parables to make the story relevant to modern-day life. When Shyamsunder once sang the Manasa song for me while unraveling his Manasa scroll, he prefaced the performance by saying that even though there are lots of different kinds of women in the country today, Behula was still a chaste wife, which I took to mean (in the Nashville sense) as a woman who stands by her man. Whether in Nashville or Naya, Shyamsunder would say, there is still need for virtue in the world, and for him Behula exemplifies those qualities.

The author at a podium in his classroom in Boston in the opening frame of Gurupada Chitrakar's scroll concerning the author's frequent visits to Naya. He named the work "Saral's Pat," Saral being the author's Bengali name.

The images included in this volume, both the old and the new, are presented to provide the reader with a broad cross-section of themes and motifs employed—religious, social, and historical—by the Patuas of Naya.

SACRED AND PROFANE

The final frame of a horizontal scroll by Gurupada Chitrakar depicting the story of how Shiva and Parvati's son Ganesha came to acquire an elephant's head. As the story goes, Shiva, here seen in white at the right, mistakenly cuts the son's head off and vows to replace it with the first one found, which just happened to be an elephant's head.

A frame from Shyamsunder Chitrakar's "Demon Wedding" executed in tribal Santali style. Here we see a blissful bride and groom being transported in a palanquin to the accompaniment of *dhol* drumming.

A scene from Jamuna Chitrakar's scroll about the goddesses Ganga (on the right in the water) and Durga (on the left with her mount, the lion) quarreling. It is common in Bengali folk religion for deities to compete against one another for the attention of devotees.

A scene from Ganga Manna's scroll about Hindus and Muslims. Ganga is the only Hindu painter in Naya. She was not born a Chitrakar, but learned to paint out of necessity when her husband, a village barber, unexpectedly fell ill and could not support the family for a substantial period of time. Now she is an officially recognized artist, even though she does not sing. Here we see Muslims performing *namaz* (prayer) on the left and a Hindu doing *puja* (worship) on the right.

Another painting by Ganga Manna, depicting Krishna's *lila* (sports) on earth. Krishna is a popular devotional deity who is an incarnation of the Hindu deity Vishnu. Known for his youthful mischievousness, we see him in the last frame on the lower right stealing the clothes of the *gopi*s (cowgirls) while they are bathing in the river. He then climbs a tree and dares them to come and fetch their clothes.

"The Funeral of Mother Theresa in Kolkata" by Rani Chitrakar. Mother Theresa, the "saint" of Kolkata, was given a televised state funeral, which inspired a scroll about her life. The refrain for the accompanying song is "Mother of the Universe, Mother Theresa; *ma*, you reside in the heavenly abode." Interestingly, she is given an appellation used for the Hindu goddess Durga, suggesting that in death she has taken on cosmic proportions. Indeed, miracles have been attributed to her since she died.

Another hagiographic scroll by Rani Chitrakar showing Sri Chaitanya Mahaprabhu (1486–1533), the founder of Gaudiya Vaishnavism, a devotional tradition originally rooted in Bengal and Orissa to the south. Known for his propagation of ecstatic chanting to Krishna, Chaitanya is considered an incarnation of Krishna. The International Society for Krishna Consciousness, better known as the Hare Krishnas, are derived from Chaitanya's theology.

Rahman Chitrakar's rendering of Ravana, the ten-headed demon who kidnaps Rama's wife Sita in the epic *Ramayana*.

R ahman's rendering of Hanuman, the super simian who is the ultimate devotee of Rama and Sita. It is he who facilitates Rama's journey to Lanka, where he does battle with the demon.

Ultimately, Rama and his brother Lakshmana slay Ravana, recover Sita, and return victoriously to his kingdom of Ayodhya, where he restores righteous rule. This is the last frame of a set of four scrolls by Rahman telling the *Ramayana* narrative.

The last register of the final frame of Mantu Chitrakar's "Satya Pir" *pat*, in which we see a man being devoured by a tiger and a crocodile as retribution for not honoring the saint by offering him *shirni*, a special sweet offered to deceased saints out of respect and reverence for them.

Another of Yama the god of death's punishments from Pabi Chitrakar's "Yama" *pat* showing what awaits those who transgress religious duty while on earth.

A frame from Manu Chitrakar's scroll on the Afghanistan War, conceived shortly after the American bombings began there. In the accompanying song, he sings the following verse: "George W. Bush got mad. A war with Afghanistan occurred. . . . Oh, hundreds and hundreds of people lost their lives. . . . Everyone should know. A strange affair."

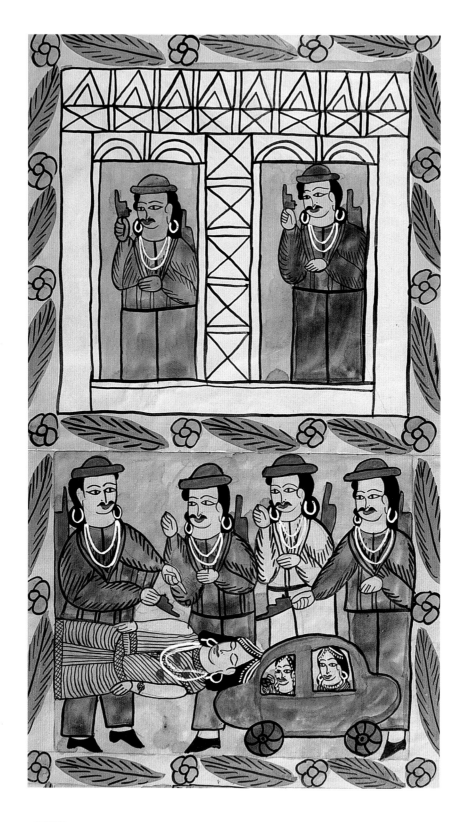

Two frames from Rani Chitrakar's scroll dedicated to the legacy of Indira Gandhi. Here we see her death depicted. In the upper frame are her two assassin bodyguards, while below we witness Mrs. Gandhi being transported in a car to a speech, at which she is shot by the two. In one poignant line, she sings, "The sky cries, the wind cries, cry the animals and birds."

"In the year 1690 Job Charnock by name, came to trade, Oh! To this charming place, in boats he came to trade," sings Gurupada Chitrakar in his commemorative scroll on the occasion of Kolkata's 300th birthday celebration. Charnock, the founder of the city, is the white figure at the center wearing spectacles.

The final frame of Anwar Chitrakar's scroll about the militant attack on New Delhi's Sangsad Bhavan. The accompanying song says that the attack was induced by the conflict in the northern state of Kashmir. Frustrated by the ongoing violence over culture and religion, the final verse reads, "Patuas wander from place to place, singing songs. From this we have learned a little something. We want our country's peace back. . . . Why don't you tell me how it'll happen? I exclaim to all. . . . India is an excellent country."

R abbani Chitrakar's "Snake" scroll. Animals often appear in *pat* paintings, and because snakes are all pervasive in tropical Bengal, they are both revered and feared. In the past, a subcaste of Patuas used to act as snake catchers and charmers. Hence, they play a conspicuous role in their lore.

*L*ike the snake, fish are quintessential to Bengali life and lore, but for different reasons. Being a dietary staple, fish symbolize wealth and prosperity. Based on a fairy tale (*rupkatha*), "Fish Wedding" tells the story of a marriage celebration in which all of the fish are invited except the big ones, who take revenge by crashing the party and eating up all of the little fish, exemplifying the proverb "big fish eat little fish." Once again, this comes from the brush of Rabbani, who is fond of painting animals.

Two scenes from Amit Chitrakar's "Forest Planning" depicting the value of coconut palms, which can be tapped for sap to make alcoholic toddy (above) and whose fruit can be harvested (below) and used for a variety of purposes in the kitchen. Amit has worked extensively with the World Wildlife Fund to create ecological awareness in rural Bengal. The accompanying song epresses the glories of nature and why human beings and the natural order are interrelated, the logic being that earth is like a mother because it nurtures our species, so we should respect and care for her in return.

Patuas often sing about natural disasters that leave a lasting effect on the nation's inhabitants, most recently the tsunami. But Medinipur was also victim to a destructive flood in 1978, which was much more devastating than the recent New Orleans deluge. In Rani Chitrakar's "Flood" we see politicians surveying the damage by air after a period of inaction. Such natural disasters are often interpreted as being brought on by the wrath of the gods. Rani sings, "Mother Ganga's play (*lila*) was like a band of demons."

The spoiled daughter-in-law, languishing decadently on a bed with too many pillows, as the old mother-in-law does the domestic chores in Jamuna Chitrakar's "1947" scroll. Jamuna sings, "Oh, daughter-in-law sleeps on a wooden cot on three pillows. Today, look, the old hag is in the threshing room mending a torn embroidery. Today, daughter-in-law oils her hair with a comb and a mirror. Today, the old hag gets a slap on the face. What else shall I say here about the state of the world?"

The world turned upside down in Mantu Chitrakar's "Earthquake."

anu Chitrakar's "Tram Journey." The scroll shows different modes of conveyance in Kolkata, ranging from horse-drawn carts and human-pulled rickshaws to buses, cars, and trams. The accompanying song praises the tram as the best way for poor people to get around because taxis and buses are more expensive, and he waits for the day when the tram will reach his village.

It is only fitting that I end this brief survey where I began: my encounter with Naya. In Rabbani Chitrakar's *pat* titled *Saraler Patua Svapna* ("Frank's Patua Dream"), I am depicted riding into the village on an elephant on the right as one of the village children takes a picture with my camera, then recording the singing of Gurupada in the lower left-hand corner.

The last frame of the same painting finds me arriving at Kolkata's international airport, and then departing in a plane to return to the United States.

A Patua's Plea

Oh rulers of our nation,
Are not the Patuas folk artists?

We draw and paint pictures and sing out the theme,
And go door to door to sell them, often reduced to
    begging.
Our art has brought us nowhere, what have we
    gained?
Oh, what is our fate?
Oh, that someone would hear!

We paint and sing, we portray the traditional life of
    our country.
Oh rulers of our nation, will you not hear?

Humans appeared on this planet,
And spoke of their need for food in sign language.
They had no words.
They ate raw meat and fish, not knowing how to
    light a fire.

Oh rulers of our nation, will you not hear?
Oh, that someone would hear!

We drew pictures on rocks and caves.
Our ink was the blood of animals.
The pictures kept the wild animals away.

Then we learned how to speak.
We continued our art on rocks and in caves.
"Come, let us go hunting together," we said.

The Patuas are spread all over India.
Deprivation and neglect is their lot.
We beg to earn our living.
Well below the poverty line, that is our lot.
Oh, that someone would hear!

We draw pictures, we sing out their contents.
We depict the ups and downs through the ages.
We paint our sorrows on the canvas.
We are not learned folk,
Since poverty cannot buy education.
Oh, that someone would hear!

We paint and we sing out their contents.
We have no place to call our own.
Never have we known a roof that is our own.
Will not those who govern lend an ear to our
    plight?
Oh, that someone would hear!

Who will hear our songs
Or wish to watch the unrolling of our pictures,
Now that radio and television have filled the homes
Of towns and villages?
Our lives remain filled with the ravages of drought
    and flood.
Oh, that someone would hear!

This is the story of our lives,
The lives of those who have no respite from sorrow
    and misery.

I, Nanigopal, make this plea.
Save us, oh save us immediately.
The art of the *pat shilpi*, the folk artist is dying a
    death.

Oh, our rulers, tell me this.
Are not the Patuas folk artists?

— Nanigopal Chitrakar, Naya village, Medinipur, West Bengal

Shyamsunder Chitrakar plying his trade.

REFERENCES

Alliance Française (ed.) 1989. *Patua Art: Development of the Scroll Paintings of Bengal Commemorating the Bicentenary of the French Revolution.* Calcutta: Alliance Française of Calcutta and Crafts Council of West Bengal.

Appadurai, Arjun. 1996. *Modernity at Large: Cultural Dimensions of Globalization.* Minneapolis: University of Minnesota Press.

Bhattacharjee, Binoy. 1980. *Cultural Oscillation: A Study on Patua Culture.* Calcutta: Naya Prakash.

_____. 1973. "The Patuas—A Study in Islamization." In S. Sen Gupta (ed.). *The Patas and the Patuas of Bengal*, pp. 95-100. Calcutta: Naya Prakash.

Biswas, Soutik. 2005. "Rural Theatre and the London Bombs." *BBC News, Calcutta.* http://news.bbc.co.uk/2/hi/world/south_asia/4748813.stm (accessed on 8/6/2005).

Bundgaard, Helle. 1998. *Indian Art Worlds in Contention: Local, Regional and National Discourses on Orissan Patta Paintings.* London: Curzon Press.

_____. 1996. "Local Discourses on Orissan Patta Paintings." *South Asia Research* 16/2:111-29.

Chakraborty, Sunil. 1973. "The Origin and Perspective of the Word 'Pat.'" In S. Sen Gupta (ed.). *The Patas and the Patuas of Bengal*, pp. 85-94. Calcutta: Indian Publications.

Chatterjee, Gouripada. 1986. *Midnapore: The Forerunner of India's Freedom Struggle.* Delhi: Mittal Publications.

Coomaraswamy, Ananda. 1929. "Picture Showmen." *The Indian Historical Quarterly* 5:182-87.

Davis, Richard. 1997. *The Lives of Indian Images.* Princeton, NJ: Princeton University Press.

Dutt, Gurusaday. 1990. *Folk Arts and Crafts of Bengal: The Collected Papers.* Calcutta: Seagull Press.

_____. 1939. *Patua Sangit (Patua Songs).* Calcutta: University of Calcutta Press.

Dutta, A. K. (ed.). 1991. *West Bengal, Census 1991, Medinipur, Part XII-B.* Calcutta: Office of the Controller.

Ghose, Bhaskar (ed.). 1973. *District Census Handbook, Midnapore*, (West Bengal, Census 1971, Series 22, Part X-A). Calcutta: Office of the Controller.

Ghosh, Pika. 2000. "The Story of a Storyteller's Scroll." *RES* 37:165-185.

_____. 2003. "Unrolling a Narrative Scroll: Artistic Practice and Identity in Late-Nineteenth Century Bengal." *Journal of Asian Studies* 62/3: 835-71.

Hadders, Hans. 2001. *The Gift of the Eye: Mortuary Ritual Performed by the Jadupatias in the Santal Villages of Bengal and Bihar, India.* Trondheim, Norway: Norwegian University of Science and Technology.

Haglund, Elisabet and Tamara Malmeström (eds.). 2003. *Sites of Recurrence*. Boras, Sweden: Kulturhuset.

Hauser, Beatrix. 2002. "From Oral Tradition to 'Folk Art': Reevaluating Bengali Scroll Paintings." *Asian Folklore Studies* 61:105-22.

_____. 1998. *Mit irdischem Schaudern und Göttlicher Fügung: Bengalische Erzähler und ihre Bildvorführungen*. Berlin: Das Arabische Buch.

_____. 1994. "Scroll Painters (*Patuya*) and Storytelling in Bengal: Patterns of Payment and Performance." *Jahrbuch für Musicalishe Volks—und Völkerkunde* 1 5:135-152.

Inglis, Stephen R. 1979. "Structural Analysis of a Bengali Folk Painting." *Journal of Indian Folkloristics* 2/3-4: 50-64.

Jain, Jyotindra. 1999. *Kalighat Painting: Images from a Changing World*. Ahmedabad, India: Mapin Publishers.

Kapstein, Matthew. 1995. "Weaving the World: The Ritual Art of the *Pata* in Pala Buddhism and its Legacy in Tibet." *History of Religions* 34/3: 241-62.

Korom, Frank J. 2006. *South Asian Folklore: A Handbook*. Westport, CT: Greenwood Press.

Kurin, Richard. 1988. "Making Exhibitions Indian: 'Aditi' and 'Mela' at the Smithsonian Institution." In M. W. Meister (ed.). *Making Things in South Asia: The Role of Artist and Craftsman*, pp. 196-210. Philadelphia: Department of South Asian Studies, University of Pennsylvania.

Larson, Gerald. 1995. *India's Agony over Religion*. Albany: State University of New York Press.

Lüders, Heinrich. 1940. *Philologica Indica*. Göttingen, Germany: Vandenhoeck and Ruprecht

Marcus, George, and Fred R. Myers (eds.). 1995. *The Traffic in Art and Anthropology: Refiguring Art and Anthroplogy*. Berkeley: University of California Press.

McCutchion, David. 1989. "Recent Developments in Patua Style and Presentation." In Alliance Française (ed.). *Patua Art: Development of the Scroll Paintings of Bengal Commemorating the Bicentenary of the French Revolution*, pp. 16-22. Calcutta: Alliance Française of Calcutta and Crafts Council of West Bengal.

McCutchion, David, and Suhrid Bhomick. 1999. *Patuas and Patua Art in Bengal*. Calcutta: Firma KLM Private LTD.

Mohanty, Bijoy Chandra. 1984. *Pata-Paintings of Orissa*. New Delhi: Publications Division, Ministry of Information and Broadcasting, Government of India.

Mukhopadhyay, Bhaskar. In Press. "Dream Kitsch—Folk Art, Indigenous Media and "11 September": The Work of *Pat* in the Era of Electronic Transmission." *Journal of Material Culture*.

Pinney, Christopher. 2004. *Photos of the Gods: The Printed Image and Political Struggle in India*. London: Reaktion.

Rao, Aruna. 1995. "Immortal Picture-Stories: Comic Art in Early Indian Art." In J. A. Lent (ed.). *Asian Popular Culture*, pp. 159-74. Boulder, CO: Westview Press.

Ray, Bisweswar (ed.). 1963. *District Census Handbook. Midnapore* (West Bengal, Census 1961, Volume. Calcutta: Superintendent, Government Printing, West Bengal.

Ray, Rabindra. 1988. *The Naxalites and Their Ideology*. New Delhi: Oxford University Press.

Sen Gupta, Shankar. 1973. "The Patas of Bengal in General and Secular Patas in Particular: A Study of Classification and Dating." In S. Sen Gupta (ed.). *The Patas and the Patuas of Bengal*, pp. 39-71. Calcutta: Indian Publications.

Sengupta, Reshmi. 2004. "Survival Tale in Titanic Times." *The Telegraph* (Kolkata) 21 February:18.

Shapiro, Gary. 1989. "High Art, Folk Art, and Other Social Distinctions: Canons, Genealogy and the Construction of Aesthetics." In R. J. Smith and J. Stannard (eds.). *The Folk: Identity, Landscapes and Lores*, pp. 73-90. Lawrence: Department of Anthropology, University of Kansas.

Shastri, J. L. (ed.). 2004. *Brahmavaivartapurana of Krsna Dvaipayana Vyasa*. Vol. I. Delhi: Motilal Banarsidass.

Siddiqui, M. K. A. 1972. "Caste among the Muslims of Calcutta." In Surajit Sinha (ed.). *Cultural Profile of Calcutta*, pp. 26-49. Calcutta: Anthropological Survey of India.

_____. 1982. "The Patuas of Calcutta: A Study in Identity Crisis." In M. K. A. Siddiqui (ed.). *Aspects of Society and Culture in Calcutta*, pp. 49-66. Calcutta: Anthropological Survey of India.

Singh, Kavita. 1995. "Stylistic Differences and Narrative Choices in Bengal *Pata* Painting." *Journal of Arts and Ideas* 27-28:91-104.

_____. 1998. "To Show, to See, to Tell, to Know: Patuas, Bhopas, and Their Audiences." In J. Jain (ed.). *Picture Showmen: Insights into the Narrative Tradition in Indian Art*, pp. 100-115. Mumbai, India: Marg Publications.

Steiner, Christopher. 1994. *African Art in Transit*. Cambridge: Cambridge University Press.

University Gallery. 1971. *Jamini Roy and Bengali Folk Art*. Jacksonville, Fl: Jacksonville Art Museum.

Varma, K. M. 1961. "The Art Medium of Saubhikas and its Nature." *Asiatische Studien* 15/3-4: 95-109.